Welfare

Second Edition

Concepts in the Social Sciences

Series Editor: Frank Parkin

Published Titles

Concepts in the Social Sciences

Welfare

Second Edition

Norman Barry

Open University Press
Buckingham

Open University Press
Celtic Court
22 Ballmoor
Buckingham
MK18 1XW

email: enquiries@openup.co.uk
world wide web: http://www.openup.co.uk

First Published 1999

A catalogue record of this book is available from the British Library

ISBN 0 335 20142 3 (pbk)   0 335 20143 1 (hbk)

Typeset by Type Study, Scarborough, North Yorkshire
Printed in Great Britain by St Edmundsbury Press, Bury St Edmunds,
Suffolk

Contents

Preface to the First Edition

Contemporary social and political thought is dominated by the concept of welfare in a way that would have surprised commentators in the last century. It is not that discourse about it was absent then. This is far from being the case since the ideas used in current political argument about welfare were first formulated at least two hundred years ago. The real difference is the central importance that is now attached to them. The injunction for the state to maximize a rather vague and diffuse thing called 'welfare', 'well-being' or 'satisfaction' now appears to override all other political values, whereas at one time this was understood to be a subordinate item on the agenda of government. Even some anti-statist writers regard well-being in some sense or other as the sole *desideratum* of existence, even though they argue that it is achieved through individual experiences rather than from direct political action. It is this that makes it a peculiarly 'modern' concept.

In this short book I have tried to outline the central features of the concept and to explicate its role in typical political arguments. Inevitably, this enterprise involves a discussion of welfare in the context of other political concepts, such as justice, equality, freedom and rights. One of the major problems is extracting it from these notions so as to isolate its distinctive characteristics. However, this is an extraordinarily difficult task because any review of welfare is certain to be overladen with highly contentious suppositions about the substantive ends of political life: the role of the state and the significance that is to be attached to individual self-fulfilment being the key areas of dispute.

I have tried to show that one of the most decisive elements in contemporary thought is the assimilation of the idea of welfare to the state. Put simply, this means that in political argument, outside more abstract political philosophy, welfare is inextricably tied up with the policies and institutions of the contemporary welfare state. However, this association is neither analytically compelling nor an accurate historical picture. Economists and social philosophers have indicated that there is a variety of sources of well-being and only in the mid-twentieth century did it become part of an intellectual consensus that political authorities should be primarily responsible for their provision. Indeed, that consensus was short-lived and in contemporary political thought we are witnessing a strident rejection by important writers of the aforementioned assimilation.

Inevitably, a consideration of welfare involves a serious analysis of the claims of individualism and collectivism. As I show in the penultimate chapter, the problem of welfare may not unreasonably be interpreted as an exemplification of these traditional and rival understandings of the social world. Furthermore, I have indicated that any discussion of welfare would be improved by an injection of scepticism, if not despair, at the possibility of reaching any resolution of the disputes that accompany the topic. This may not matter so much at the conceptual level, but in the area of practical politics, the intractability of the concept has generated insoluble policy problems. Thus, many welfare 'measures', emanating from individualist or collectivist sources, have spawned malign consequences, unanticipated by their authors. It is only slightly comforting for the contemporary sceptic to be told that many of the contemporary problems to do with social policy are, in fact, replays of events that have taken place throughout the history of governmental involvement in the promotion of welfare.

Nevertheless, my account is not primarily historical. I have not tried to present a chronological account of the development of the idea of welfare but have concentrated on contemporary issues and debates in the context of the values and moral precepts that have prevailed in the concept's intellectual biography. Thus, there is no reference to Tom Paine, whose *The Rights of Man* contained the germ of the modern welfare state, but a lot about the utilitarians – precisely because it was their justificatory framework that predominated in the long-term validation of welfare and the welfare state.

Again, there is little or no factual material in the book. There is a plethora of statistical studies of welfare and welfare institutions, drawn largely from the USA and Britain, but much of it is of an ephemeral nature. It seemed to me much more important to present an overall picture of those concepts, ideals and values that have in the present and the past suffused political discourse about this contentious subject. I have no doubt that the same theorctical and ideological material will be found equally serviceable in the future.

The bulk of the manuscript was written at the University of Buckingham and I am grateful to Elizabeth Stewart and Lizzie Clayden for their excellent typing. However it was completed at the Social Philosophy and Policy Center, Bowling Green State University, Ohio, and I am indebted to that institution for its excellent facilities for research. I would also like to thank Mary Dilsaver for doing the final secretarial work at short notice.

Norman Barry
Bowling Green, September 1989

Preface to the Second Edition

A lot has happened in the welfare world since this book was first published in 1990. What I have tried to do in this second edition is to elaborate on some conceptual points that were left incomplete in the first edition, and to continue some lines of enquiry that were broached then. Thus the postscript contains a slightly more detailed analysis of need, and related ideas, than was in the first edition. But perhaps more important, I have taken up the debate on the welfare state that was already underway in the 1980s. The institutions and policies of welfare have been under considerable critical analysis both in the USA and in Britain and I have developed some of these ideas. What is significant is the revival of a moral approach to thinking about welfare. This has had as serious an impact on classical liberal theories of welfare as it has on more collectivist approaches. It is unlikely that the welfare state in most Western democracies will survive in its present form. It is hoped that the following pages provide the reader with an insight into the theoretical reasons for contemporary changes. I would like to thank my research assistant, Faye Marchant, for her skilful and thorough work in the preparation of this edition.

Norman Barry,
Buckingham, January 1998

The Idea of Welfare in Political Thought

I

In contemporary political and social thought the concept of welfare is perhaps undergoing its most thorough examination ever: an intellectual interrogation which is being carried out from a variety of ideological persuasions. The causes of this enquiry are both immediate and long term. The immediate cause is the current dissatisfaction with one particular application of welfare philosophy – the 'welfare state' – and the more permanent source of contention is the appropriate place, and moral ranking, of the welfare ideal alongside other evaluative notions such as justice, equality, freedom and rights.

It is important at the outset to distinguish between the concept of welfare and that array of social and economic arrangements and public policies collected, for convenience, under the general heading of the 'welfare state'. It is so for at least two reasons. First, a critical attitude to that version of the welfare state characteristic of most contemporary democracies does not entail the rejection, or even doubt the relevance, of welfare to a fully articulated social philosophy. Indeed, some sceptics of the welfare state might well argue that many of its typical features, e.g. its alleged paternalism, coercion and inefficiency, are themselves destructive of a proper concept of human welfare. Second, the welfare state, because it is merely a set of institutional arrangements, conceals or dissembles a whole complex of evaluative principles: nobody (surely) values the arrangements for their own sake, whatever virtues they have must be a function of their role in the advancement of more general and ethically appealing human goals. The concept of welfare had been the subject of philosophical argument between political theorists and economists a long time before the main institutions of the welfare state were forged in the early part of this century.

Yet, nevertheless, it cannot be denied that the current argument about welfare has been occasioned largely by the disenchantment with the post-war welfare state felt by many social theorists, both from the radical 'New Right'[1] and the Left. Although it would be an exaggeration to say that there is a 'crisis' in the system (it has too many intellectual defenders and too much popular support to be in danger of an early dismantlement), the contemporary discussion over its structure and purpose is part of the much wider debate that is going on in political and social thought. Specifically, the question of the proper role of the state in economic and social life has been analysed as never before during the post-war period and some older notions (such as the 'nightwatchman state') have been disinterred from the grave, to which it was assumed they had been confined forever, resuscitated and made serviceable for intellectual debate about social policy.

Again, the most analysed concept in social philosophy, that of justice, has been inextricably bound up with welfare. The whole notion of the welfare state has often been justified in terms of a concept of justice that is specifically redistributive: it defines fairness not in terms of an allocation of economic resources tied to individual entitlements under the procedural rules of legitimate ownership but as a complex set of institutions designed to take account of 'needs' and 'deserts' that transcend claims based on private property.

These are simply two examples of the intense argument over public policy, and its foundations in ethics and political economy, that have emerged from the breakdown of the so-called 'consensus' that ruled Western democracies since the Second World War. Such was the dominance of this consensus over intellectual life that it led to the claim that we had reached the 'end of ideology',[2] that there were no substantive differences of principle that divided people so that intellectual effort should be invested in piecemeal improvements to an existing, agreed-on 'paradigm'. The consensus included specific responsibilities of government (responsibilities that had been obliquely recognised before but never fully articulated). They were the maintenance of full employment through intervention in the market with the use of macro-economic policies (demand management), the provision of a generalized welfare system operating *outside* both the market system and private charity, and the promotion of social and economic equality through nationalization and redistributive taxation.

What is interesting about the British experience of the consequences of the breakdown of this consensus is that the institutions of the welfare state have survived more or less intact, and with the level of public expenditure remaining more or less the same despite the vagaries in the rate of economic growth. This, in the face of a clear divergence in views about welfare and the successive election victories of a Conservative Government (1979–92) whose rhetoric, especially that of its leadership, was sceptical of the idea of welfare encapsulated in the post-war paradigm. This can no doubt be partly (or mainly) explained by the presence in the system of strong inhibitions to change: so many legitimate expectations have been built into the institutional arrangements, the guarantee of pensions being one obvious example, that it would be impossible to inaugurate substantial reforms without making considerable numbers of people worse off. This problem itself is as much a problem of welfare philosophy, involving crucial conceptual problems of fairness and legitimate expectations, as it is of practical politics.

What is significant about the welfare issue in contemporary political life is not so much the changes that have taken place in policies but the nature of the debate itself. The respective theoretical positions adopted, notably those in the familiar 'market versus the state' argument, have a very long history so that in many policy areas we are witnessing a replay of intellectual battles fought in the last century. A spectacular example is the current debate between those individualist social theorists who believe that all extra-market payments should be in cash (the famous Negative Income Tax) and those who claim that they should be tied to specific welfare services (education, health, housing, pensions, and so on) and not easily obtainable. Advocates of the former maintain that cash payments have the singular merit of preserving freedom of choice and individual autonomy whilst the opponents claim that this system simply encourages profligacy and a 'dependency culture' precisely because its benefits are treated as *entitlements*. But this is, in fact, another version of the argument at the turn of the eighteenth century over the infamous 'Speenhamland system' of outdoor relief and its alleged defects, an argument that was *politically* resolved with the introduction of the Poor Law (1834) system, which had the precise aim of making welfare difficult to obtain and accompanied by a certain amount of stigma.

Again, and from a somewhat different perspective, the current justifications for state welfare that make use of the notions of 'community' and 'citizenship' are echoing some familiar late nineteenth-century social philosophies. There was a definite revulsion (experienced in a particularly convoluted way in the thought of T.H. Green[3]) against that individualism of classical liberalism which identified the citizen as merely an abstract agent, endowed with a set of legal and political rights, who owed no obligations to society other than the recognition of the equal rights of others. In this view, a person's welfare was simply a function of the voluntary exchanges made with others via the inviolability of contract. Citizenship was then exhausted by its legal features, and the entitlements that flow from these. The contemporary theorists of citizenship are echoing Green in their claim that the notion extends beyond the idea of a mere judicial relationship to include claims on the economic resources of the community by virtue of membership of it and an identification with its goals.

The objection to markets from the citizenship school is not merely that an exchange system, inhabited by anonymous maximizers, may fail to produce the general welfare (however defined) but that, in a moral sense, it cannot produce an autonomous agent. A person who cannot make his way in market society, and therefore has to rely on charity, cannot be fully a citizen. Thus even if voluntary donations were sufficient to alleviate hardship, the very fact that they were gifts from one stranger to another and not valid claims *in justice* from the community, is sufficient to disqualify the recipient from full membership of society. Implicit in all this is a rejection of – or at least a sceptical comment on – Sir Henry Maine's famous observation that progress is exemplified by the 'movement from status to contract'.[4]

II

The above specimen arguments have been implicitly about state welfare but, as has been suggested earlier, it would be a mistake to identify all arguments about welfare with the relative merits and demerits of compulsory provision by political authorities. The concept has a use outside this context. Indeed, it would be a gross misdescription of the history of political thought to say that it was solely concerned with welfare. It seems to be a feature of 'modernism' that social and political theories are evaluated or ranked by reference to how they deal with welfare, or what welfare-enhancing policies in a material sense, can be derived from them. This is as much true of individualist, market-based social theories as it is of collectivist ones. Whatever their differences, they seem to be united in their belief that the object of social philosophy and public policy is to make people 'happier' or more prosperous – that a state of well-being is that at which governments should aim, either by intervening very little, or by managing a substantial part of people's lives.

Nevertheless, not only is it not the case that welfare has to be understood in a purely material sense but also, and more importantly, the maximization of welfare, however defined, is not necessarily the sole desideratum of political philosophy. It is surely more consonant with the common usage of political terms to see welfare as one of a plurality of political concepts, with intuitively no greater claim to priority over justice, rights or political order itself. Again, it is difficult to see why welfare maximization should be the overriding concern of government. Unless the virtue of welfare maximization is attached to all desirable forms of human activity (in which case the concept becomes trivial or even redundant), the welfare theorist must indicate why it is valuable and in what relationship it stands to other human values.

The difficulty in contemporary political argument, however, is that whereas at one time welfare might plausibly have been contrasted with, for example, justice and individual rights, those latter ideals have very largely (and some would say erroneously) become tied to welfare itself. This conflation is especially characteristic of theories justice. Whereas Adam Smith could write, in 1759, that 'justice is, upon most occasions but a negative virtue, and only hinders us from hurting our neighbour,'[5] such an account of justice that showed so great an indifference to well-being would be highly controversial today (although some writers, such as Hayek and Nozick, do proceed in this manner, and are for that reason highly controversial). Smith would only countenance the use of force to guarantee the rules of negative justice, but welfare philosophy sanctions its use to bring about a redistribution of resources. Exactly the same is true of rights. At one time they were regarded as claims to forbearance from invasive action by others but they are now more likely to be regarded as entitlements to well-being from the state. And, of course, the idea of *positive* liberty, a definition of freedom which requires that certain economic resources must be made available to individuals if their actions are to be properly called free or uncoerced, is necessarily tied to a collectivist theory of welfare.

This apparent promiscuity of welfare, a concept which attracts itself somewhat indiscriminately to other moral and political ideas, is the cause of some confusion in political argument. It is not true that a rejection of the association, say, between justice and welfare, implies also that welfare should be rejected as a political principle. It is surely analytically more accurate to say that the welfare principle is but one of a plurality of principles that are operative in political argument. This disentangling of welfare from other values should not be seen merely as some sanitizing process, a necessary cleansing exercise whereby our political language is purified so that value disagreements can be more easily identified. It also has a more substantive implication. This is that the assimilation of other values to the welfare ideal imposes upon a society an agreement about values, an hierarchy of ends and purposes which is unlikely to exist.

In the history of political and moral philosophy the explanation and justification of other human ends and purposes has usually taken precedence over the demands of welfare: indeed, the idea that some notion of well-being or sensual satisfaction, experienced either by individuals through market exchanges or delivered to society or other 'aggregates' by collective action, should be any kind of evaluative criterion, is a comparative latecomer. In ethics, the claim that there are certain moral duties that hold irrespective of our inclinations and desires has had an equally firm grip on our moral sentiments. This appears to be the case in European thought. Whether such duties are a product of Christian natural law (as in the Thomist tradition) or demonstrable by a liberal conception of reason (as in the Kantian tradition) is less important than the fact that both distinguish ethics from all notions of material well-being. Whatever its derivation, there has been, and still is, a tradition in normative ethics and politics that does insist that the claims of the 'right' have a greater claim on our reason and sentiments than the welfare imperative.

Also, in Western political thought, the explanation of the conditions for social order has been of greater concern to theorists than the maximization of welfare. Thus although Hobbes derives a theory of the authoritarian state from individualistic premises, in which the 'good' is identified with subjective desires (a metaphysic which was to be adopted by later welfare theorists), his major concerns were political obligation and the theories of law and sovereignty. Another example would be Edmund Burke. In a specific reference to the supposed economic and welfare responsibilities of the state, he maintained that governors 'cannot do the lower duty, and in proportion as they try it, they will certainly fail in the higher'.[6] In both those writers, the claims divert attention from more fundamental political concerns.

What is then peculiarly modernistic about welfare philosophy is the elevation of what many writers such as Burke have called the 'lower responsibilities' of government to a position equal in importance to the preservation of law, order, continuity and social cohesion. Following on from this is the almost natural claim that government action is condemnable should it fail to meet the demands of the welfare imperative. From this perspective the roots of the welfare philosophy are primarily utilitarian: the value of welfare measures is obviously linked to certain sorts of consequences. The consequences may not always be calibrated in terms of pleasure, as Benthamite utilitarianism seems to require, but it is to consequences of some observable kind that welfare philosophy is addressed. For this reason, welfare philosophy is ineluctably concerned with questions of economics and public policy and only marginally about law and political obligation.

However, the references to 'well-being', satisfaction and other familiar expressions in welfare philosophy are by no means uncontroversial.[7] It seems to be the case that the arguments in welfare philosophy are characterized by intractable disputes about people's needs, wants and interests so that even if it were agreed that the maximization of welfare should be the goal of public policy, there is likely to be little or no convergence on what features such maximization would display.

Of crucial importance in the history of welfare thought is the question of whether well-being or satisfaction should refer solely to individual experiences (a subjectivist individualist position) or whether we can make legitimate evaluations of aggregate phenomena, 'society', 'state', and so on, in terms of welfare. Of course, societies and 'states of affairs' are evaluated and compared according to some welfare scale but there has always been doubt about the legitimacy of such comparisons. This doubt arises for at least two reasons.

First, many individualist thinkers adhere to a strict ontological position. This holds that, in reality, only persons are capable of experiencing well-being and that propositions containing collective terms are merely shorthand expressions for complex statements about individual sensations. This does not, of course, exclude a public dimension to public life since for various reasons (to be explained in Chapter 4) individuals may only be able to satisfy their desires through *public* rules. But even here the legitimacy of the public activity is only a function of its consistency with some procedure that maximizes individual choice. This position, closely associated with welfare economics, would not preclude a welfare state, provided that this emerged from a choice procedure which was itself legitimated by individual preferences.

Secondly, and the following point is intimately connected to the first, is that comparisons between various 'states of affairs' in terms of their welfare-enhancing properties invariably involve an interpersonal comparison of well-being – something that is forbidden by a dominant tradition in welfare economics. An interpersonal comparison of individual well-being involves an observer making a judgement about how a particular policy affects two or more people. It was a major feature of classical utilitarianism that such comparisons could be legitimately made. For example, it was maintained that progressive income tax was a scientific way of maximizing utility (welfare) on the ground that a redistribution of income would hurt the rich less than it pleased the poor.[8] The assumption here is that everyone's taste for money income is the same, i.e. increasing amounts bring proportionately decreasing satisfactions. But, of course, this assumption may not be true; some people may be hurt more than others by a fall in their money income, so that the redistribution will have to be justified on ethical grounds rather than because it maximized 'objective' utility. Since almost all redistributive policies channelled through the welfare state make some people worse off, the connection between 'welfare' as understood by welfare economists and what is ordinarily meant by welfare (at least by moral and political theorists) is not very close.

Nevertheless, there is a very strong welfare judgement or evaluation implicit in the whole tradition of liberal economics from Adam Smith. It is that an unhampered market system, or *laissez-faire*, powered by self-interest, will spontaneously generate a state of affairs superior to any known alternative: an array of goods and services that reflects people's subjective choices. Its virtue is said to be that it depends on a small number of uncontroversial assumptions about human beings, notably that individuals are the best judges of their own interests and that competition between producers will ensure efficient production. However, almost all writers in this tradition, including Smith himself, believe that there are circumstances in which this is not so, that there are certain sorts of goods and services which, although 'wanted', are not supplied in the marketplace: they are 'public goods'. The debate is about the nature and extent of public goods.

There is then a real disjuncture in welfare philosophy between those writers who maintain that the only welfare improvements are those that come about through individual exchanges in the market or through a public-choice mechanism that generates outcomes (public goods) that are desired by individuals but unavailable in the market, and those who interpret the welfare imperative in a collective sense: that there are social values that ought to be promoted independently of individual choice. In this latter view, aggregate entities are compared in terms of how deprivation is alleviated, and of how much equality is promoted: the apparatus of the welfare state is specifically charged with the function of promoting those objective goods. In the former view, however, the state is merely a mechanism or a conduit for the transmission of individual preferences for certain public activities. Of those public goods, law and order, defence, clean air and so on, are the most familiar but the transmission of individual preferences for public welfare would, of course, not be excluded. Indeed, it is claimed that this is the only way in which a welfare state can be justified.

It is true, though, that the non-individualist tradition in welfare cannot ignore institutional factors either. It may be possible to ground the claims to welfare in some morality involving equality, social justice, and even rights, as justificatory criteria but the delivery of whatever goods are thought to be welfare goods does involve crucial institutional questions. Unless welfare services are to be designed and implemented by an omniscient and benevolent dictator, a position adopted by no theorist of the welfare state, some account must be taken of the institutions which are responsible for welfare. One good example is the problem of equality, for it has been frequently shown by egalitarian economists that the supply of such services as education, health, pensions, aid to home ownership and so forth, typically results in outcomes favourable to middle-income groups.[9] Even in collectivist welfare states, decisions are always in some sense subjective, and therefore analysable in terms of self-interest and the other features of human action.

III

The welfare imperative implies, in a broad sense, that public policy ought to be directed towards increasing the well-being or satisfactions of persons (taken individually or collectively): it makes no ethical difference whether that is a *negative* policy of refraining from the free play of market forces or the state acting positively in the belief that the exchange system cannot generate all that is desirable. But it may be the case that welfare can be provided outside both the market and state – through voluntary gifts. Indeed, altruism has been endorsed by conservative and classical liberal thinkers as a major, if not the only, part of a welfare programme. The duty of charity figures prominently in nineteenth century literature and social philosophy and it is claimed that a free society fosters both self-interested market motivations and altruistic sentiments. Even Left-wing thinkers, such as R.M. Titmuss,[10] have recommended the 'gift relationship' as the ideal form of human social concern, independent as it is from the non-tuistic motivation of capitalism and the coercive, and often unreliable in welfare terms, power of the state.

This is a crucially important point, for it is not often appreciated that the modern democratic welfare state depends very much on a form of altruism, i.e. the non-selfish predispositions of the voters. It cannot be assumed that the state is a 'neutral' body that will automatically provide a level of welfare decreed by a welfarist ethic. A prominent egalitarian and welfare thinker, R.H. Tawney, wrote, of the state, that: 'Fools will use it, when they can, for foolish ends, criminals for criminal ends, sensible and decent men will use it for ends which are sensible and decent'.[11] In a democratic society the state must, in theory, be used to advance the 'ends' of its citizens and the success of the welfare imperative will depend on the spread of the non-tuistic sentiment across the voters; and, it should be added, on the efficiency of the particular democratic machinery in transmitting that sentiment. There is therefore a genuine comparison to be made between the effectiveness of the market and the state in the mobilizing of the welfare disposition. How can Tawney ensure that the state will be used for 'sensible ends'?

It should be noted in this context that the classical liberal's justification for state welfare depends upon a kind of altruistic sentiment: the preferences that, it is assumed, most people have for the relief of deprivation. It is only because of a 'public good' problem in the provision of welfare, i.e. the contribution *each person* makes to the relief of indigence is so negligible that there is little incentive to donate, that the state has to step in and correct 'market failure'. State welfare then becomes a curious form of 'enforced altruism'.

An emphasis on welfare as the relief of poverty, and the mobilization of the altruistic impulse, may be seen as a way of uniting the conventional Left and Right of the ideological spectrum, a drawing together of superficially disparate political predispositions into a common programme. Indeed, it may be called a rationalist approach to welfare: a conviction that there is an ultimate agreement about social ends and that those disputes that remain are about the means of achieving them. It is assumed that those latter disputes are resolvable by rational methods.

However, this may be somewhat misleading, a false assumption that there is agreement over the nature of a concept which is inherently contestable and characterized by intractable arguments about individuals and their relation to society. It could be maintained that the welfare 'problem' is not exhausted by a rational consideration of the question of efficiency, i.e. of merely solving the problem of deprivation. Throughout the history of the welfare debate there is a theme of communitarianism and (to some extent) citizenship that recommends a form of welfare society: a vision of a social order that is not merely characterized by rational deprivation-alleviating institutions and policies but by the fostering of intimate communal bonds. In this view, an efficient welfare state that rested entirely upon individualistic assumptions would itself be divisive; its institutions would 'separate' human agents[12] from each other whereas a welfare society would join them in a common enterprise. In this conception of welfare society equality, for example, would be valued as much for its communitarian-enhancing effects as for its specific deprivation-reducing role (if it has any, which many welfare theorists deny).

IV

It is the case that the welfare debate has historically been suffused with the question of individuality and the problem of individual responsibility for action. Outside the sphere of formal welfare economics, where individualism is exhausted by the problem of translating private choices into preferences for public goods, the question of evaluating the effects welfare policies and institutions have on the person is crucial. It is a major claim of welfare state sceptics, especially in the USA and the UK, that indiscriminate welfare payments, especially if they are in the form of entitlements requiring no reciprocal obligations on the part of recipients, have an enervating effect on individuality and personal responsibility. They create what is popularly known as a 'dependency' culture rather than a society of responsible, autonomous agents.

There is, however, a further reason to note the connection between welfare and the ideas of responsibility and causality. While the philosophy of the nineteenth-century Poor Law stressed that indiscriminate welfare should be strongly discouraged because its attractions would cause people to become dependent on the state, there was an equally influential nineteenth-century welfare tradition which argued that people were entitled to relief precisely because they could not be held (morally) responsible for the predicaments in which they might find themselves. Thus it was held that the movement of the trade cycle, which produced periodic spells of unemployment, and other large-scale economic phenomena over which individuals obviously had no control, justified a welfare state. It was not fecklessness (which it was said would be encouraged by extensive state welfare) that produced deprivation and indigence but an unhampered market itself. It was not therefore individual responsibility that was significant but the powerlessness of the individual in the face of irresistible social forces. J.A. Hobson wrote (in 1896):

'Only upon the supposition that environment affords equal opportunities for all can we possess a test of personal fitness. Then only
should we be justified . . . in attributing the evil plight of the poor
or unemployed to personal defects of character'.[13]

It is difficult to overestimate the importance of the connections
between causality, personal responsibility for action and the concept of welfare. For how those ideas (and the interaction between
them) are understood has a crucially important effect on attitudes
towards state involvement in economic and social matters. For
example, many liberal theorists simply deny the causal connection
between the operation of the free market and the existence of
(avoidable) social deprivation. Indeed, they attribute much of this
to mistaken government policy itself: the existence of periodic mass
unemployment is said to be caused by mistaken monetary policies
that generate business cycles, and homelessness and inadequate
housing is understood as a consequence of inhibitions, such as rent
control, to the supply of rented accommodation. In the absence of
such misguided interventions, it is claimed that the market would
generate social welfare. Furthermore, although they concede that
the minimum level of state-supplied welfare that they would permit
might have the effect of inducing irresponsible behaviour they
would refrain from making a *moral* judgement about this: indeed,
they cannot, given their assumption of self-interest as the major
motivating force in human behaviour.

On the other hand, there is a strong tendency in much of state
welfare thinking to overlook the causal explanations of undesirable
social phenomena. Thus the existence of forms of deprivation itself
constitutes a *reason* for therapeutic action by political authorities,
irrespective of the cogency of a rational explanation of how such
phenomena could have occurred. That is why some of the interventionist measures seem to be counterproductive: they exacerbate
the problems they are designed to solve. A familiar argument is that
the virtually costless availability of certain social benefits encourages the size of the benefited group to grow – it is sometimes
known as the problem of 'moral hazard'.

V

This brief overview of the concept of welfare reveals it to be an
extraordinarily complex political value. Although there might be

some minimum agreement that it is that concept which describes well-being, satisfaction, the relief of deprivation (in contrast with those whose concern is with duty, political obligation and order *in general*) beyond this we enter a realm of almost irresolvable dispute. What is 'well-being'? Can it be measured and is it possible to compare rationally the rival political programmes that are designed to maximize it? What is its connection with justice and freedom?

Perhaps the most difficult and intractable dispute is over the range of issues and human concerns which are appropriate for welfare policy. The classical liberals, the originators of serious discussion about the concept, limited its range to those satisfactions experienced by individuals in market exchanges, supplemented by the production of necessary public goods. This included carefully-defined measures to alleviate poverty. Yet it is doubtful if the latter would include education, pensions, unemployment insurance, health and housing as public responsibilities, as they are so regarded today. The rationale for their inclusion is perhaps the most vexed of current welfare issues. Although the welfare state is justified normally in redistributive terms it is by no means unanimously accepted that redistribution is its only rationale. It is also maintained that the collective delivery of the familiar welfare services has efficiency properties. That is to say, *everybody* would gain from the collectivization of certain services, because of inherent defects in the private market. For example, although healthcare is not technically a public good which can only be provided by the state, there are some facts about it, notably the problem of consumer ignorance, which establish a prima facie for public involvement.

There is then a series of questions to be asked of welfare. Some are to do with the *ultimate* aims of welfare (and are quite probably incapable of definitive resolution), others are almost technical, concerning the most efficacious means to agreed ends. But, however fresh the issues in the contemporary debate appear to be, it is important not to lose sight of the fact that they are not at all new but are as old as welfare itself.

Utilitarianism and the Origins of Welfare Philosophy

I

The history of welfare thought is inextricably bound up with welfare institutions. This is not to say that there is an exact correspondence between ideas and policies (although there are some examples of institutional arrangements, illustrated in a spectacular way by the English Poor Law system as amended in 1834, which do seem to have been the product of rational design) but only to suggest that movements of opinions and ideas have an important influence on the formulation of public policy. Some of the connections between ideas and policy are rather puzzling. Nineteenth-century Britain, for example, witnessed the curious phenomenon of the rise of collectivist welfare institutions (although the welfare state itself is really a twentieth-century concept) grafted on to an economy which was conducted under more or less *laissez-faire* principles. There is a welfare imperative implicit in *laissez-faire* economics but it is not that associated with the idea of the welfare state.

It is undoubtedly the case that modern ideas of welfare derive from important developments in economics and social science that began towards the second half of the eighteenth century, particularly the rise of utilitarianism. However, the connection between utilitarianism, *laissez-faire* economics and welfare is a subtle one and is the source of many confusions. The most damaging of these is the too-ready assimilation of Benthamite utilitarianism to what has come to be known as liberal welfare political economy. For although it is true that Adam Smith and Jeremy Bentham were both advocates of the market economy (whether Smith was a genuine *laissez-faire* theorist is a matter of some dispute) their foundations for it are subtly different and have divergent policy implications. It is no exaggeration to say that Benthamite activist utilitarianism is the intellectual source of that bureaucratic form of state welfare that was to dominate public policy in nineteenth-century Britain. It is rationalistic and contrived, and the state has a welfare role the features of which can be precisely delineated.

On the other hand, the welfare tradition that derives from Smith is non-rationalistic: beneficence is a product of spontaneity and not 'reason'. The major innovation of Smith was his demonstration of how those natural coordinating mechanisms of the market (price signals) encouraged self-interest to operate benignly and for the public good. This public good was an accidental outcome of self-interest rather than the product of a rational plan. There is no suggestion that the public good can be structured on a scale of observable utilities and no implication that society had a welfare function that could be implemented by benevolent dictators.

Adam Smith was not the first social theorist to understand the public welfare as an (almost) accidental outcome of the baser motives. Bernard Mandeville (1670–1731) in a more dramatic, and perhaps more compelling, way had shown in his *Fable of the Bees* (1720)[1] that the promotion of the traditional virtues of abstinence and self-restraint were destructive of public welfare. That, indeed, commerce and virtue were antithetical and that art, prosperity and progress are only possible if men's natural desires (especially avarice) are given full reign. Hence his observation of the bee-hive in its non-moral state: 'Every part was full of vice/Yet the whole mass a paradise.' This is the origin of the radically subversive liberal individualist doctrine that, if welfare is the goal to be strived for, it will come about through the following of our natural passions rather than through deliberate prosecution. It is a sentiment that is echoed in contemporary *laissez-faire* thinking (Milton Friedman is in some important respects a modern Mandevillian) and is to be contrasted with that other tradition which understands welfare as a product of morality (of public-spirited governments and enlightened citizens).

To a modern welfare theorist, even if it were true that an unhampered market functioning through price signals did produce an equilibrium, this would satisfy only a part of his programme. For this would be to interpret welfare in efficiency terms only and to ignore the distributive questions that naturally arise in this context. Yet Smith's welfare economics are indifferent to distributive justice. As he wrote in *The Theory of Moral Sentiments*: 'Mere justice is, upon most occasions but a negative virtue, and only hinders us from hurting our neighbour'.[2] It is true that a market exchange system requires basic rules of justice, in the guaranteeing of which it is permissible to use force, but they function like the 'rules of grammar' only. Smith does concede that a society founded upon such rules may not be particularly virtuous, and that the exercise of benevolence would transform a mere commercial society into a more pleasing social order, but it would be a part of a supererogatory morality (i.e. not compelling) rather than strictly obligatory. It is this feature that recurs constantly in liberal thought: economic welfare and distributive justice are strictly separate. That whatever needs are left unmet by an efficient market must be catered for by a variety of charitable institutions (including the state acting as one type) rather than in the form of justiciable entitlements. The rules of justice are there to service a commercial society and the major (although not the sole) duty of political authority is to maintain them.

Smith's social philosophy anticipates the major elements of the contemporary classical liberal's approach to welfare, not merely in his refusal to countenance any notion of social justice, but also in his explanation of the mechanics of the production of economic well-being. It is from human nature itself – 'the uniform, constant, and uninterrupted effort of every man to better his condition' – that we are to expect improvement. This is so for at least two reasons: the limitations of human knowledge and the interest and virtually uncontrollable tendency to prodigality on the part of government.

Smith's antirationalism is an important intellectual weapon in his argument against the idea that we ought to invest government with the responsibility of promoting well-being. Although he tends to view the market pricing system as a signalling device for the efficient allocation of resources rather than as a device to coordinate necessarily dispersed information, a point that was to be developed later with great sophistication by Hayek, the general tenor of his argument points in this direction. The rationalist forgets that 'in the great chess-board of human society, every single piece has a

principle of motion of its own, altogether different from that which
the legislator might choose to impress on it'.[3] In other words, the
rationalist works against the grain of human nature and fails to
appreciate that the exercise of 'natural liberty' itself is all that is
required to make the best use of limited resources. As Smith
pointed out, that selfishness that lies behind the famous metaphor
of the 'invisible hand' has itself an unintended beneficial consequence for *social* welfare. After all, the more concerned people are
about their selfish interests the less they will be dependent on
others.

The objection to government is simply a particular application of
the universal self-interest axiom. In a direct anticipation of modern
public choice theory, Smith maintained that self-interest was as
much a feature of public as it was of private action.[4] The public
good was primarily an accidental product of each individual's striving: 'By pursuing his own interest he frequently promotes that of
society more effectually than when he really intends to promote it.
I have never known much good done by those who affected to trade
for the public good'.[5]

Individual striving can and does lead to inequality: Smith often
comments on this and on one occasion even suggests that the original rationale of law and government was to protect that inequality. However, and again in anticipation of modern liberal welfare
theory, he argues that it is acceptable precisely because it helps the
poor better than any other known system: even the worst-off in
commercial society were far more prosperous than the tribal chiefs
of a savage society.[6] Furthermore, there is an implicit faith in the
presence of the so-called 'trickle down' effect of market society, i.e.
the expenditure of the rich leads ultimately to an increase in the
well-being of the poor. As Mandeville had earlier said: 'Many
things which were once looked on as the invention of luxury are . . .
counted so necessary, that we think no human creature ought to
want them.'[7]

Thus although Smith's ethics and political economy were ultimately utilitarian it was a utilitarianism of a kind quite distinct from
that activism which is associated with Bentham and his legislative
heirs in the nineteenth century. There is no 'welfare function' for
society as a whole which reason can determine, no uniform scale of
happiness by which we can calibrate political action, but only a collection of anonymous and self-seeking individuals loosely held

together by market signals and the simple rules of procedural justice.

Yet Smith is by no means completely immune to the allure of the republican ideal. The quintessential idea of a liberal society, i.e. that people can be held together in the absence of common (or communal) purposes and little direct political activity, could be said to begin with Smith's thought but he also recoiled more than a little at the prospect of the full development of that delicate embryo.[8] He had reservations about the commercial society; for despite its prosperity, it could have malign effects on people's capacity for a full participation in moral and social life (the problem of 'alienation'). This scepticism about the long-run future of commercial society has two implications for modern welfare.

The first relates more to the almost technical question as to whether an exchange system driven only by individual desires can produce all that individuals want (the complex question of how we can know what it is that individuals desire in the absence of a market was to be explored by later liberal welfare theorists). In a famous passage Smith revealed his concern with the problem of market failure. When writing on the functions of government he argued that (in addition to law and order) there was the duty

> .... of erecting and maintaining certain public works and certain public institutions, which it can never be in the interest of any individual or small group of individuals, to erect and maintain; because the profit could never repay the expense to any individual or small number of individuals, though it may frequently do much more than repay it to a great society.[9]

In the economist's sense of the word, welfare is not maximized by pure exchange since there are desirable things which cannot be priced by the market. There is here, then, the germ of the modern theory of public goods, but what Smith does not consider is the institutional machinery for their delivery or what criteria there are for isolating genuine public goods. Modern welfare state theorists have expanded the range far beyond what he had in mind.

II

It was Jeremy Bentham (1748–1832) and his followers who first annexed the notion of welfare to ethics, who poured scorn on the

idea that ethical value could be located in the concepts of duty and
right conduct detached from immediate consequences, and made
possible (theoretically at least) the release of justice from its
moorings in the idea of rules and rule-following so that it could be
made to serve the supreme end of human happiness. Furthermore,
in his writings, the idea of welfare takes on that specifically
aggregative form that has become its modern hallmark. Thus
although Bentham described 'society', 'community', and so on as
'fictitious entities' which had meaning only when resolved into
their component parts – individual feelings and sensations – this
was something of a verbal carapace beneath which thrived a
fiercely aggregative doctrine. For it is undoubtedly the case that
once the individual's preferences are known to an observer, that
individual is subsumed and conflated with others into a social
utility function. It is by this collective criterion that competing
policies are to be evaluated and divergent societies compared.
Hence Bentham's oft-quoted, and thoroughly ambiguous claim,
that: 'It is the greatest happiness of the greatest number that is the
measure of right and wrong.' Policies were justified solely in terms
of whether they had a tendency to 'augment the happiness of the
community or diminish it'.[10]

Yet the intriguing question is: how is it that a social doctrine
which superficially is entirely concerned with beneficence, that
charges government with the responsibility of 'augmenting happiness' became associated with, in the popular mind at least, a rigid
doctrine of *laissez-faire*? – a normative theory which regarded the
provision of social welfare by the state as a mere adjunct (which
was necessarily harsh) to the welfare naturally generated by the
market. Again, how is it that a utilitarian theory of justice that in
principle was forward-looking in the sense of being about the creation of future happiness (rather than backward-looking in its
concern with the enforcement of impartial rules) led to no significant redistributive policies? It is notable that what we *now* understand as the welfare state owes very little to Benthamite principles.
Indeed, the philosophical theories of welfare that emerged in the
late nineteenth century, which not only sanctioned an enlarged role
for the state in social welfare but also justified a significant shift
in the form of its delivery, were written in defiance of those
Benthamite principles that had validated earlier legislative
intervention. By the year 1900, Benthamite principles in their

application to social welfare were regarded with considerable opprobrium by enlightened social thinkers.

A further difficulty in Bentham's welfare theory is the apparent paradox that, from the same principle of human motivation as Smith, self-interest, he could construct an economic theory significantly more *laissez-faire* than that of the author of *The Wealth of Nations*, and a social and legal theory that sanctioned a centralization and extension of state power which would have been regarded with anathema by that same author.

Thus in his *Defence of Usury* and *Manual of Political Economy*[11] Bentham refuted on *laissez-faire* grounds a string of interventionist measures that Smith had justified: they included the navigation laws, the public provision of roads (at zero price), a national coinage, a public postal system and legislation to enforce a maximum interest rate. In his arguments here Bentham was a more rigorous exponent of the liberal axiom that 'each individual knows his own interest best' than Smith (this was especially so in relation to his belief in a completely free market in interest rates) and a perceptive advocate of the economic virtues of risk-taking and entrepreneurship. Yet in his *Constitutional Code*[12] we find a firm commitment to state welfare via the Poor Law, and support for legislation controlling conditions in factories and an argument for public works – not for the public goods reasons, but as devices to cure unemployment. Furthermore, there is within Bentham's philosophy a primitive statement of the doctrine of the declining marginal utility of money income: a notion that was used by later utilitarian writers to sanction (theoretically) significant redistributive welfare policies on the ground that they maximized social utility.

These paradoxes are apparent rather than real and can be resolved once the logic of Benthamism is understood. What is crucial to this is a distinction between a natural and an artificial harmony of interests. Self-interest would produce a natural harmony in normal markets but elsewhere the 'legislator' was required to provide surrogate incentive structures to bring about order, the criminal law being an obvious example. Individuals were everywhere governed by the psychological imperative to seek pleasure and avoid pain so that to implement the 'general happiness' required that some precise measurement of pain and pleasure be made.

The difference between Benthamite utilitarianism and that of Adam Smith turns partly on the possibility of there being a rational way of distinguishing between natural and artificial phenomena. Smith saw coordinating processes everywhere, including (and especially) the common law process of adjudication, so that the need for legislative intervention was minimal. Bentham, however, envisaged a sovereign legislature charged with the function of creating happiness. Indeed, all law emanates from the sovereign; a free action is simply that which is permitted by the legislature, and a fully rational sovereign would permit only those free actions that would maximize observable utility (welfare). This then is the theoretical background from which sprang the Benthamite legislator, frenetically seeking improvements on natural systems.

But do we know what an 'improvement' is? Do we have an objective measuring rod of happiness, equivalent to the temperature gauge on a thermometer? For the Benthamites, it was not merely pleasure but a 'sum of pleasures' which is important and it is here that the aggregative, indeed collectivist, elements become paramount and the errors of crude Benthamism manifest. For surely pleasure is a subjective thing inhering in each individual and incapable of the precise calibration that rational welfare legislation requires? Thus when we say that the community is 'better off' through the adoption of a welfare policy, we are not saying anything cognitive at all but merely uttering some subjective opinion. There is no 'scientific' way of making the interpersonal comparisons of utility that such judgements require.

This problem has bedevilled the history of welfare economics, liberal or otherwise, for even those theorists who oppose the idea of a 'welfare state', as it is understood conventionally, face exactly the same problem when they justify *any* collective provision of goods and services, such as defence, law and order and so on, that are supposed to reflect people's choices. In the early versions of Benthamism, the implementation of the collective welfare was the responsibility of a 'benevolent dictator' (and this is implicit in many versions of utilitarianism) but as Bentham himself realized, such a person is no more immune to the push and pull of pleasure and pain as other individuals. A meaningful notion of a collective welfare judgement, which is at the heart of Benthamism, seems as remote as ever.

Nevertheless, Bentham's inconclusive struggles with this issue highlights a fundamental feature of welfare policy. That is, there is an ineradicable element of subjectivism in all decisions about welfare. If we say that welfare is maximized through the market, this must mean that it is individual sensations that are the determinants of well-being, i.e. the criteria by which we are to assess states of affairs. On the other hand, if we argue (surely, plausibly) that the market system leaves legitimate welfare desires unsatisfied, what they are, and the extent to which state action should be used to satisfy them, is a subjective decision arising out of some collective choice procedure or from that of an élite (as, for example, it is in Fabian welfare theory).

It is not obvious that all utilitarian welfare theory requires us to evaluate various collective 'end-states', i.e. configurations of wealth, income, well-being, and so forth, in terms of their measurable welfare-enhancing properties. Although Adam Smith was a utilitarian, and although he certainly argued that the workings of the (metaphysical) invisible hand produced a social outcome better than conceivable alternative forms of economic arrangement, this outcome is qualitatively different from that envisaged by orthodox utilitarianism. Its features cannot be known in advance of the operation of the exchange system itself. Thus despite the use of such phrases as the 'public interest', the rationale of the market is not that it produces any such 'knowable' outcome or final state, but that it coordinates human action and provides that minimal level of predictability which individuals need to secure their own well-being.

The itch to reform, intervene and correct the failings of the market is therefore absent in that line of liberal welfare thinking that emanates from Smith but is omnipresent in that which proceeds from Bentham. What we notice in the latter is the argument that welfare somehow depends on knowledge: not the implicit or tacit knowledge that is dispersed in the interstices of market society, but the knowledge that a centralized legislator requires to effect an immediate improvement in social well-being.

This distinction is of paramount importance for the current welfare debate. For the heirs of the Benthamite tradition, whatever their ideological persuasions, are united in their belief that a market failure is an aberration that can only be solved by immediate remedial action by a fully-informed legislator: the assumption is that the exchange process has few self-correcting processes, either for the production of wanted public goods or for the relief of indigence.

III

It is with those points in mind that we can resolve the apparent
paradox mentioned earlier: the co-existence in the nineteenth century of a more or less decentralized *laissez-faire* economy and a burgeoning set of highly centralized welfare institutions (though it did
not constitute a welfare state). Furthermore, a brief consideration
of the intellectual history of this period shows how it is that the
apparent egalitarian (albeit muted) motif of theoretical utilitarianism had no effect whatsoever on practical welfare policies.

It is in the intellectual controversy surrounding the Poor Law in
England, and especially in the thought and career of Sir Edwin
Chadwick,[13] Bentham's secretary, that we find the rationale for the
co-existence of *laissez-faire* economics and social welfare. But the
issue is not of historical interest only, for the principles that were
invoked in it have a universal influence and are, indeed, at the heart
of some of the welfare debate today. The nineteenth-century utilitarians saw the relief of poverty as a kind of public good: we would
all benefit from its absence but, given the principle of human nature
(primarily self-interest) with which utilitarianism operates, this was
unlikely to occur spontaneously. It is also pertinent to observe that
the desire to alleviate poverty was as much a function of the fear of
a threat to social order that might occur from large numbers of
able-bodied paupers as it was of an altruistic sentiment. In fact the
former, somewhat cynical, consideration has been a covert feature
of some contemporary liberal welfare thought. The latter sentiment
was probably reserved only for the physically infirm. The welfare
problem was not something that could be left to spontaneous processes: it required the artifice and skill of government to solve. Yet
its resolution also required the skill of the social scientist in unfold-
ing laws of cause and effect and the gathering of relevant empirical
data.

The danger of indiscriminate welfare payments was that they
must have a tendency to encourage individuals to become welfare
claimants: a good or service provided at zero price will attract an
infinite demand. In fact, it is almost impossible to design a welfare
scheme which will not have this effect. This is, of course, by no
means a knock-down argument against all state welfare since the
protagonists can say it is a price well worth paying for the relief of
suffering, or they can simply ignore it. Nevertheless, it was the

predominant theme of utilitarianism and classical economics. The designers of the English Poor Law scheme of 1834 produced the most daring and controversial solution to this problem. Some writers, however, notably Malthus and Ricardo, opposed the Poor Law, largely because they were convinced that it would exacerbate the population problem and because it was inconsistent with the logic of classical economics. But Chadwick and others were determined to mitigate its ill-effects while still leaving welfare as a legitimate government responsibility.

The prevailing welfare arrangements[14] (deriving from the Elizabethan Poor Law) were inefficient largely because of, in the eyes of the utilitarians, their local nature. The major aberration was the payment of outdoor relief, dramatized in the famous Speenhamland system (1795), not merely to paupers and the physically infirm *but as a supplement to those already in employment.* The rationale for this was probably a combination of sentiment (an appreciation of the cyclical nature of employment) or simply fear of riots if it were stopped. But the system was an affront to utilitarianism: not just in terms of the costs it imposed on local rate-payers but its inconsistency with the science of human nature. The payment of a supplement to the badly paid had a distorting effect on wages: it encouraged employers to pay less.

Whether Chadwick's enquiries (he was Secretary to the Poor Law Commission) revealed accurate results, in fact later economic historians have doubted that the system of outdoor relief had the malign effects that its critics maintained,[15] is not strictly relevant. What is pertinent to the philosophy of welfare is the solution that was proposed, or rather, the principles from which it was derived. In an effort to discourage people to become indigent, outdoor relief was abolished (though, in practice, it remained in some areas) and relief to the able-bodied only given in workhouses, under supervision. In economic conditions, it was deliberately designed to be worse than for those in employment.

This was the infamous 'less eligibility' principle – the obverse of outdoor relief, which made the person in receipt of benefit more eligible. It was argued in the Poor Law Report that: 'Every penny bestowed that tends to render the condition of the pauper more eligible than that of the independent labourer, is a bounty on indolence and vice.'[16] So began one of the most notorious administrative regimes in British social history. A subject of obloquy for its

harshness, deliberate deprivation, attenuation of liberty, centralized administration and exclusion of a portion of the population
from citizenship by virtue of their indigence alone. Yet it was not
without its able defenders at the time, many of whom had benevolent and humanitarian instincts. John Stuart Mill thought it 'right
that human beings should help one another; and the more so in proportion to the urgency of the need',[17] but he was as anxious as
Chadwick to ensure that the system was not so attractive as to
encourage the evil it was designed to cure. It was to observers at
the time an ideal adjunct to *laissez-faire* economics because, while
dealing with a problem that the market apparently could not
handle, the phenomenon of avoidable indigence, it operated
through the same mechanisms, the resistible pull and push of pleasure and pain. The regime of the workhouse was an administrative
surrogate for the price signals of the market.

The whole system of the amended Poor Law represents the scientific side of utilitarianism. But what of the ethical injunction that
governments are to be appraised in accordance with their capacity
to promote the 'general happiness' when a system, the new Poor
Law, seemed to be designed to exclude some from its enjoyment?
What of utilitarianism's alleged indifference to personal morality in
the context of a regime of control apparently dedicated to the inculcation of desirable values? Furthermore, the allure of that covert
principle of *social* justice implicit in Bentham's *sotto voce* approval
of the equal diminishing marginal utility of money principle seemed
quite resistable.

In fact the kind of welfare outlined is perfectly consistent with
this brand of utilitarianism, which is as much a tribute to the
ambiguity of the doctrine as it is to the virtues of the Poor Law
scheme. The greatest happiness of the greatest number was
certainly guaranteed by it. In fact, although Bentham interpreted
the phrase a vague summing up of all interests in society, Chadwick treated it as a name for a kind of engineering efficiency. Individual liberty had no intrinsic value in utilitarianism; it was no
more than a provisional claim in the calculation of a social utility
function. Finally, redistribution implied in the diminishing marginal utility principle was never taken seriously as a policy goal by
Bentham or his followers, including its most sophisticated
exponent, F. Edgeworth, precisely because its implementation
would be a threat to prosperity and security. Nevertheless, it is the

one doctrine within classical utilitarianism that has survived in some form or other.

Ultimately, of course, there is no conflict between ethics and science for the convinced utilitarian: it is a theory of the *organization* of welfare more than anything else. There is no 'right' to welfare since there are no 'rights' independently of positive legislation anyway in utilitarianism.

Yet before this whole approach is summarily dismissed we should remember that the utilitarian social theorists located some depressing features of the human condition that have persistently recurred, to the embarrassment of more optimistic and generous welfare theorists. They demonstrated that there is an intimate connection between the proposals for welfare (that may well have a persuasive normative foundation), the theory of human nature that must underlay any 'science' of welfare and its policy proposals, and the institutional arrangements that are recommended for the delivery of welfare. Thus it is that the critique of certain contemporary welfare policies which are said to create a 'dependency culture', a citizenry who lose their self-reliance and autonomy precisely because of the ease of welfare, and its distribution in the form of 'entitlement', is redolent of that 'Speenhamland versus the new Poor Law' debate which preoccupied much of Victorian thinking on social issues.

IV

The utilitarian concern with welfare in the nineteenth century of course extended way beyond the question of the Poor Law. What is characteristic of almost all of the reforms that it sanctioned was that they were, it was claimed, consistent with the market. The welfare problems that arose were not normally thought to be caused by the markets; the identification of a welfare problem as an inevitable outcome of *laissez-faire* was to be made later by social philosophers with a rather different ethical social and economic value system. To utilitarians, these problems were said to derive from impediments to the smooth functioning of the market, often of a political kind, or from the presence of correctable 'externalities'. The latter obviously included public health and sanitation problems that accompanied rapid industrialization and which preoccupied Victorian reformers. The universal human characteristic of self-interest, and fundamental 'laws' of classical economics, scarcity, supply and demand, diminishing returns and so on, were still thought to be impregnable and unsurmountable obstacles to the kind of extravagant social welfare proposals of the burgeoning socialist movement.

Yet, curiously, the work of two writers already mentioned, Chadwick and John Stuart Mill, was already undermining the theoretical structure of the liberal political economy of welfare. In their very different ways both provided intellectual ammunition for later assaults on the structure of ideas, practices and institutions which they, in principle, were concerned to defend. Chadwick's contribution to the undermining of the market's claim to be a welfare-enhancing institution was his licensing of state action on the ground of *efficiency*, and that of Mill was his admission of the concept of social justice into the litany of classical liberalism.

Chadwick's political economy represents in canonical form the act-utilitarian public administrator. He had an almost entrepreneurial alertness to market failure and an optimism about the capacity of government to make welfare improvements which stands in marked contrast to Smith's scarcely concealed cynicism about politics. Thus in addition to the Poor Law reforms, Chadwick was the mastermind behind the centralized management, control and regulation of police, public health and water supply, and railways. His rationale for such regulation by reference to market failure was a direct anticipation of modern welfare economics, which is very largely limited to this. Inefficiency was a product of private monopoly, wasteful competition or the market's failure to supply wanted goods at all.

Mill's quasi-democratic sentiments and his veneration for freedom put him at odds with the centralizing predilections of some utilitarians, yet he too produced a social philosophy of welfare that anticipates much of modern thinking. Although he worked with the grain of human nature and had little time for utopian schemes that ignored the teachings of classical economics, his vision of a humane social order had significant egalitarian overtones.

What is important here is the rationale for this view. It can be found in the enunciation of a famous principle in his *Principles of Political Economy* (1848) concerning the limits of government action on an economic order. He wrote that:

The laws and conditions of the production of wealth, partake of the character of physical truths. There is nothing optional or arbitrary in them. This is not so with the distribution of wealth. That is a matter of human institution only.[18]

Thus although political intervention could not alter the output of an economy, this depended upon the productivity of labour and capital and so on, it was within the capacity of government to distribute it according to those moral principles it deemed appropriate. This has been much criticized by liberal political economists since it presupposes a false distinction between production and distribution, as if any distribution rule could be chosen with there being no effect on output. Yet, of course, particular distributive rules will have a feedback effect on production, e.g. economic welfare will be reduced by heavy progressive taxation (though there might still be compelling normative reasons why it should be introduced). Mill did in fact suggest that we could have a scientific measure of the effects of the distributive principles that we choose, but he never explored the implications of this insight for his original distinction.

Mill undoubtedly favoured some form of social justice, most notably equality of opportunity.[19] He still insisted upon the efficiency of the market and the justice of its *results* but only if access to it were made more equal. Hence, his distrust of progressive taxation, which 'punished' success and his advocacy of inheritance taxation which, he claimed, made for a socially desirable wider spread of wealth. Irrespective of the merits of Mill's recommendations, his alleged distinction between production and distribution, and hence qualified approval of social justice, is germane to twentieth-century welfare philosophy. The reason is that, unlike the welfare schemes of Chadwick which were entirely about efficiency, the modern welfare philosopher, like Mill, is as much, if not more so, concerned with distribution.

Anti-individualism: From the Minimal State to the Welfare State

I

Despite the growth of state institutions to relieve indigence in the nineteenth century and the emergence of social theories that seriously challenged the hegemony of an unsullied individualism, there was neither a welfare state nor a philosophy to validate even an hypothetical one. There were, of course, in literature as well as social theory, fierce attacks on *laissez-faire* and exposures of the poverty and misery associated with rapid industrialization which, it was alleged, that economic system created. It is true that in Germany, under Bismarck, there had been forged the first systematic state system of social welfare, including old-age pensions and social insurance, which became something of a model to be imitated elsewhere. It is also true that in that same country there had developed an 'historical' school of economics which challenged the purported universalism of classical economic theory, the individualistic postulates on which it rested, and the anti-interventionist bias which those presuppositions generated.

In Britain, however, 'welfare' was still a word that was used to describe individual experiences and whatever state aid existed was seen as an adjunct to the market, supplied because of a fear of social unrest from an alienated pauper class, or as a consequence of the altruistic motives of other individuals. The idea of a welfare state, a comprehensive set of institutional arrangements which understood needs as entitlements that flow from membership of a community, was yet to find a firm theoretical and political foothold. Liberty was still by and large interpreted in a negative sense, i.e. a person's freedom was a function of the absence of laws or other (alterable) human impediment: lack of resources did not count as a constraint, and each individual was assumed to be the best judge of his own welfare. From the latter point it followed that personal responsibility for action was paramount so that a distinction could be made between the deserving and the undeserving poor.

Perhaps the decisive break came with the reversal of the explanation of the process of social causation, and the consequent effect this had on the idea of personal responsibility that had been a feature of nineteenth-century thought. The emergence of the case for the welfare state began with the argument that, instead of public welfare being the cause of dependence, loss of autonomy and capacity for individual responsibility for action, and the market the source of independence and freedom, the opposite was the case. The advocates of the welfare state were able to argue that the individual had little or no control over his destiny in the context of impersonal market forces: the market system was unpredictable so that the Victorian ideal of self-sufficiency was not achievable for some groups. It followed from this that, since people could not be held responsible for their plight, the foundations for welfare had to be quite different from those associated with utilitarianism. Adam Smith's natural liberty principle began to be interpreted in a much less benign way than it had been by even the later, more interventionist utilitarians.

The birth of the modern theory of welfare depended on the re-interpretation of certain key political concepts: notably, liberty, community and equality. The effect of this re-interpretation was to transform the nature of society from a conception of a loosely co-ordinating set of individuals bound together by common rules but lacking a common purpose, into a more intimate form of order (a 'community'). If people were held together by social bonds that transcended contractual relationships, then they could make claims on each other, as citizens of a common enterprise, which could exceed their contributions as measured in more calculative, economic terms. From this perspective, state welfare would cease to be regarded as an act of charity but a form of entitlement.

A key concept in the development of welfare thinking is liberty.[1] Utilitarians tend to work with a concept of liberty that identifies free action with action that proceeds from subjective choices unrestrained by (alterable) impediments, notably laws backed by sanctions. Freedom is analytically separated from power and economic conditions so that the existence of poverty itself, or where conditions in the labour market were such that a person had little alternative but to accept low wages, would not count as restrictions on liberty. Restrictions on liberty were linked with the intentional acts of persons, e.g. legislators. It would not be impossible to justify state welfare within this conceptual framework but such intervention would not count as freedom-enhancing. Indeed, to the extent that interventionist welfare legislation attenuated freedom of contract, it would be paternalist. By accepting state provision, the individual gave up some liberty, which was surely the thinking behind early welfare legislation, such as the Poor Law.

However, if it can be shown that acts that appear to derive from subjective choice are in reality compelled, although the compulsion is from social and economic conditions rather than statute laws or identifiable human agents, then welfare legislation, to the extent that it alleviates harsh economic conditions, also enhances liberty. Thus if (alterable) economic conditions have the effect of causing a person to act in a certain way, precisely because there is no viable alternative course of action, then that person's *autonomy* is thereby reduced: the fact that the choices are subjective is either highly misleading or irrelevant. If this is so, the appropriate conceptual framework must now encompass a harmony between welfare, autonomy and liberty. State action to relieve indigence enhances liberty as autonomy. This contrasts strongly with classical liberal welfare economics which, in its endeavour to be 'scientific', accepts all choices *qua* choices as uncoerced, irrespective of the circumstances of their origin. In its more stringent versions, it disqualifies itself from comment on the distribution of property rights from which choices are made.

II

The redefinition of liberty underlies much of modern thinking but its intellectual roots are to be found in Idealist social philosophy dating from T.H. Green (1836–82), and continuing through the work of his followers, B. Bosanquet (1848–1923), D.G. Richie (1853–1903) and L.T. Hobhouse (1864–1929), and often known as the 'New Liberalism'.[2] Although the connection between it and specific welfare policies may be tangential, and in Bosanquet's case we find a marked hostility to modern welfare institutions and policies, New Liberalism's redefinition of liberty and its recasting of the notions of citizenship and community have provided, almost unwittingly, ethical foundations for the modern interventionist state. In effect, the community becomes a source of value independently of the subjective preferences of atomized individuals.

In his famous essay, 'Liberal Legislation and Freedom of Contract' Green gave a definition of liberty which admirably summarized the position:

> . . . when we speak thus of freedom, we should consider carefully what we mean by it. We do not merely mean freedom from constraint or compulsion. We do not mean merely freedom to do as we like irrespectively of what it is that we like. We do not mean a freedom that can be enjoyed by one man or one set of men at the cost of a loss of freedom to others. When we speak of freedom as something to be so highly prized, we mean a positive power or capacity of doing something worth doing or enjoying, and that, too, something that we do or enjoy in common with others.[3]

Although Green was specifically talking about factory legislation, compulsory education and landlord and tenant law, the metaphysic espoused here has a relevance to the wider welfare sphere. For here liberty is not subjective choice, i.e. individuals responding to the dictates of desire and aversion but the exercise of a power and capacity to act in concert with others. It is the image of there being a common good apart from the caprice of momentary, ephemeral desires that is important. If there is such an objective source of value, then to restrain an employer, for example, from making a momentarily satisfactory but exploitative contract with an employee, would in fact liberate the employer as well as the employee. Similarly, to intervene in the pursuit of the common good would be to increase the autonomy of citizens rather than coerce them or treat them in a paternalistic manner. The unrestrained market, on the other hand, divides and abstracts the individual from his community. And indeed Green does not subscribe to a doctrine of untrammelled *laissez-faire* in social and economic philosophy: 'The freedom to do as they like on the part of one set of men may involve the ultimate disqualification of many others or of a succeeding generation for the exercise of their rights.'[4] Again those rights are not universal rights of an abstract self, but those that are embedded in the community.

However, in practical terms, Green does not endorse in any real sense a welfare state. The state is interpreted repeatedly as a 'hinderer of hindrances' to the achievement of the good life rather than the positive provider of conditions of well-being. Although, in principle, his identification of individuality with community had heavily statist, and even authoritarian, overtones there is no expansive positive programme of political action in his work. The implication is that individual morality via communal action is more nearly realized in *voluntary* welfare work. Indeed, Green's followers were heavily engaged in social work in the deprived areas of London and instrumental in setting up the Charity Organisation Society.

Green's province was morality rather than politics and economics and his theoretically expanded concept of the state yielded little in the way of positive welfare proposals: indeed, his reverence for private property, albeit on morality enhancing rather than efficiency-enhancing grounds, provided a barrier to redistribution and social justice. However, what was of importance later was his restatement of the principles of social cooperation. He just did not accept the liberal utilitarians' claim that competition in the marketplace, a terrain inhabited by self-interested anonymous individuals, could produce a benign, even, cooperative outcome. Competition and cooperation remained antithetical and continued to be so in welfare state thought. Adam Smith's 'natural liberty' became submerged by a curious mixture of diluted German organic metaphysics and Victorian moralism. Nevertheless, his conception of a common good that remained somehow objective, and flourished as an ideal independent of the spontaneous outcome of individual striving, became an ethical standard of welfare which survives today.

Certainly, his most immediate disciple, Bernard Bosanquet,[5] had no difficulty in harnessing the notion of an organic state, whose foundations are utterly non-individualistic, to a rigid anti-state welfare ethic. His objection to welfare, including the Poor Law, was derived from the notion of individual moral development which is integral to Idealist social philosophy. For in this, moral responsibility is absolutely crucial and any policy that hindered this was condemnable for that reason alone. Thus in Bosanquet there is no attempt to relate deprivation to causal economic factors outside the individual's control: it is a consequence of causal factors internal to the individual, i.e. fecklessness, indolence and moral underdevelopment. These would only be exacerbated by indiscriminate state welfare. Such views, of course, owed nothing to individualism and indeed, Bosanquet had no objection to state coercion outside welfare. The briefest acquaintance with Bosanquet's work shows that Idealist and organic theories of society do not necessarily produce a welfare ethic.

Yet an alternative to *laissez-faire* did develop from these sources (although they were not the only ones) and attention did shift perceptibly away from the question of moral responsibility towards the justification of the supply of state welfare to the indigent, irrespective of how their predicament came about. This is the quintessentially modern idea behind the welfare state: its concentration on *need* itself regardless of its causes, or of the particular consequences that may flow from attempts to relieve it. If we add to this the demand for minimum incomes and redistribution in the name of social justice, we get the ideal of a citizenship. This is not defined by civil and political liberties alone but also includes claims to economic resources, not as a market-determined reward for work but as a consequence of the membership of the kind of community described by Green.

The philosophical anti-individualism of Green was given an interpretation more congenial to positive welfare action by the state in the work of writers such as the aforementioned Richie and Hobhouse, and also the economist J.A. Hobson (1858–1940). What was surprising is that these writers added an *evolutionary* gloss to the organicism of Green, a rather surprising addition since Herbert Spencer had already become notorious for his use of the 'survival of the fittest' doctrine to condemn the growing welfare interventions as antithetical to social progress (as well as rights-violating).[6] However, evolution was now given a progressive twist. It became the description of a process away from the individualism of *laissez-faire* towards the re-integration of the individual into the community: welfare and socialism were not only desirable, they were the directions in which society was moving.

However, the persuasiveness, and the effectiveness with regard to welfare, of those new liberal ideas derived not from evolution but from the particular proposals that they made and the use made of empirical studies of the capitalist economy. This was especially true of the economist, Hobson, who made much of the argument that a capitalist economy was inherently unstable, that its randomness made nonsense of the Victorian imperative of individual responsibility and whose side-effects made a welfare state a necessity. Hobson, like the Fabians, was convinced that he had refuted old liberalism by facts, argument and reason: unemployment, for example, was an inevitable product of chaotic, unplanned capitalist systems. Unrestrained capitalism would not show a Smithian tendency to equilibrium but to a despotism of the financiers.[7]

L.T. Hobhouse, in two works especially, *Liberalism*[8] (1911) and *The Elements of Social Justice*[9] (1922) first put a recognizable welfare philosophy, encompassing equality, income redistribution and a positive role for the state, into the context of the new communalism or collectivism. Philosophically, questions about liberty could not be divorced from serious consideration of the economic environment. Liberty necessarily involves the full development of the human personality (as opposed to the mere absence of restraint) but this elaboration was incoherent without a proper conception of equality: 'liberty without equality is a name of noble sound and squalid result'.[10] Significant inequalities, which the state has a moral duty to correct on behalf of the collective good, turn individual liberty into a power that some have over others.

Equality actually meant equality of opportunity: since liberty itself was linked to opportunity, the full development of personality for each person required resources. In fact, Hobhouse saw wealth in a functional, communal way, and its justification depended on its contribution to that common good which we all shared. Hence 'functionless' wealth, e.g. in the form of land ownership and inherited resources, was appropriate for redistribution in order to increase equality of opportunity.[11] It follows from this that the prevailing Poor Law system, because it is a last resort for desperate individuals, and permits individuals no opportunities beyond survival, could not contribute to their well-being in the fullest sense. Therefore, Hobhouse was a firm believer in a minimum income (*not* paid only to the unemployed and destitute and not to be considered as an act of charity) and the legitimate inclusion of 'need' into the calculus of welfare considerations.

What emerges from these abstract and philosophical enquiries is that the theory of the modern welfare state derives very largely from an enquiry into the alleged inadequacies of the individualistic market order rather than from a fully-fledged socialist or Marxist theory. These latter views do not therefore argue for a welfare state separately from the theory of socialism itself. Indeed, some social-ists, and all consistent Marxists, have to regard the typical welfare institutions as in a very real sense harmful because they are struc-tured on a pre-existing capitalist order. Their thriving would be inimical to the future aim of abolishing the capitalist order. Thus the minimal aims of redistribution encouraged by the new liberal-ism would be a distraction from the real inequality which was an intrinsic feature of the capitalist system itself. Indeed, in theoreti-cal Marxism, since the state is defined in essentialist terms as a coer-cive force to protect class interests, any welfare role that social theorists might attribute to it must be illusory. Almost all overt socialists saw welfare as a form of social control, as indeed it was.

Thus it is that the intellectual foundations of the welfare state do not sanction the abolition of the market but an amendment of its defects: to point out that its remorseless allocative efficiency was incapable of attending to objective needs since its domain was the realm of subjective choice. The welfare state was grafted on to a market which was always liable to produce outcomes which, although unintended, offended morality. Thus it is that the Fabians, and the famous survey of poverty by Rowntree, provided empiri-cal support for the claims of ethics and social philosophy. The emphasis was moving away from causal explanations of indigence, and the attribution of moral responsibility, towards the identifi-cation of need. In the work of the Fabians,[12] the moral factor is not ignored: it is argued that (alterable) social conditions create the moral problems that so concerned previous welfare thinkers. What is perhaps of more importance, however, in the Fabian approach is that the solution to the welfare problem is considered to be a matter of expertise – and bureaucratic expertise at that.

The attention to statistical detail and the a priori reliance on cen-tralized institutions for the delivery of welfare is redolent of the earlier utilitarian approach, however much the two schools may have differed in substantive conclusions (especially over the viabil-ity of *laissez-faire*). The 'citizenship' ethical rationale for welfare is less apparent in Fabian thought; regulation, control and the specific organization of preventive measures are much to the fore. It should also be noted that the social science to which the Fabians were addicted was of the factual, data collection kind and less concerned with the explanation of laws, especially of the causal type found in economic theory. A consideration of the implications of those, notably the recognition of scarcity and the insatiability of human wants, might well have dampened the enthusiasm of the reformer for the kind of *wholesale* welfare implied by the new theory.

The social measures that were introduced by the radical Liberal Government (elected in 1906) reflected many of these concerns. Compulsory education, and its financing by the public purse, had already been established on the assumption that individuals could not provide it for themselves, although this assumption was by no means proven and has recently been seriously challenged. Non-contributory old-age pensions were established in 1908. Although the system contained some conditions and grounds for disqualification, it was structured round a genuinely collectivist principle that dissolved the distinction between the deserving and the undeserving poor. The National Insurance Act 1911 had more of an individualist foundation since its benefits (sickness and unemployment) depended upon contributions. It was compulsory, and this offended against individualist principles. Yet, it was justified because of its theoretical actuarial basis. This gave it some of the features of a 'public good', i.e. that the state could spread the risks and so provide a technically efficient welfare service. However, economists of an individualist persuasion have always denied that compulsory national insurance is a genuine public good and, indeed, the history of insurance-based state welfare services is a record of the gradual but persistent whittling away of their actuarial base.

III

Although in the political theory of welfare the rationale of interventionist measures is couched in terms of ultimate ethical principles – social justice, equality, needs and rights – there are certain secondary considerations, maxims one might almost say, which tend to govern the organization of welfare itself. But these organizational principles are not merely technical devices, agreement on which can be expected to come from all rational people. They are themselves subject to as much dispute as the more overtly ethical values. The kinds of arguments that occur here are the following:

- Should welfare be delivered 'selectively' to those in need or 'universally' as claims that individuals make of each other as members of a common social enterprise?
- Should they be in kind or cash?
- Should they be organized on basic insurance principles and properly funded on a sound actuarial basis or treated as simple redistribution?
- Should they be given some special constitutional protection or left to the regular voting procedures and pressure group bargaining of democratic politics?
- Lastly, and perhaps of most importance, should the welfare state be understood as a 'safety-net', a minimum of guaranteed wellbeing, for those unable to survive in market society or is the idea of market society itself antithetical to welfare (*pace* the liberal economists)?

Only recently have these problems received any serious theoretical treatment and the practical measures that have been introduced by government represent responses to the exigencies of the moment rather than legislative enactments of rational schemes. The development of welfare thought, outside the technical sphere of welfare economics, is something of a curious and often incoherent and confused dialogue between ideas and institutions.

A major factor in the development of twentieth-century welfare philosophy was the experience of mass unemployment and the growing assumption that only government could alleviate it. In the last century, the very concept of unemployment was unknown and the idea that government could correct it unthinkable. However, the experience of the Great Depression in the 1930s and the acceptance of the idea of *involuntary* unemployment linked welfare ineluctably to the management of the economy so as to secure full employment (macro-economics). No longer could indigence be exclusively linked to moral failing, and the notion of personal responsibility for action seemed to have a limited application in the context of apparently uncontrollable and random economic forces to which almost anyone was potentially vulnerable. The idea that welfare was a form of charity, to be delivered to a small minority, at subsistence level and governed by strict rules, seemed senescent. The events of the time seem to endorse the philosophical idea of a community whose bonds of intimacy transcended the liberal society of anonymous individuals held together only by contract. Most important of all, perhaps, was the acceptance of the theory that 'distribution' no longer meant simply the distribution of income to labour according to its marginal productivity (the classical liberal's theory of wages) but redistribution (at least some) away from this according to ethical criteria, such as need, desert and so on, or even equality for its own sake. Thus it was that social welfare became inextricably tied to 'social' justice.

It is perhaps somewhat surprising that America should have made tentative moves towards the modern welfare state: moves that were almost entirely pragmatic responses to the Great Depression of the 1930s. Of particular significance was the Social Security Act 1935, whose primary, but by no means only, purpose was the introduction (by the *federal* government) of retirement pensions. This legislation, aside from the constitutional issues peculiar to America that it involved, is important because it is an early illustration of one of those 'secondary' problems of state welfare mentioned earlier. Should compulsory welfare payments be subject to sound actuarial principles or simply redistributive? In fact, American social security was originally intended to be properly 'funded' by contributions but very quickly it ceased to be so: it developed into a form of 'entitlement' irrespective of contributions.

However, it is in the Beveridge Report (1942)[13] and the legislative enactments that followed it, that we see the variety of inchoate welfare principles at work. By identifying five major categories of suffering – want, disease, ignorance, squalor and idleness – the Beveridge Report established a virtually unlimited role for the state in welfare. Taken in conjunction with the commitment to Keynesian macro-economic policies, the idea of welfare had become completely associated with a social philosophy designed not to replace the market but to correct it where appropriate. Adam Smith's natural liberty was not eliminated but restrained by the firm leash of the state. Again the necessity for intervention was linked to causal analysis, but this time it seemed to be of a particularly sophisticated kind. Keynesian macro-economics theory, with its alleged demonstration that there was no natural tendency for the market to equilibrate at the full employment of all resources, seemed to rest the welfare function of the state on scientific grounds.

Theoretically, this became the consensus view on welfare in

Britain in the post-war era. Yet it did not derive from a coherent social theory: there were elements of citizenship theory, social justice, Fabianism, interventionist economics, and even some of the behavioural features of market economics. It continued to rely upon the insurance principle, i.e. individuals were compelled to contribute to a national fund out of which they were paid entitlements in times of emergency. Yet the 'need' factor was recognized, most notably by 'supplementary benefits', to be paid to those not covered by insurance. The system did recognize the 'rights' of citizenship in that redistribution was not seen as an act of charity, as in the Poor Law, but as a consequence of membership of the community. The egalitarian features of the Beveridge Report were limited to the provision of a 'safety-net' for the indigent and it showed its belief in normal market incentives in the following remarkable passage: 'the gap between income during earning and during interruption to earning should be as large as possible for every man'.[14]

There was a variety of welfare schemes spawned by the basic principles implicit in the 'Beveridge Revolution', and other countries, notably Sweden, produced similar and sometimes more egalitarian measures. In the last forty years or so the extent of state welfare has widened considerably in all Western democracies and the various changes to particular services, and their financing, have become so complex that it would be impossible to document them here. The disputes that they generated were mainly about the secondary welfare considerations mentioned above.

What is significant about the growth of the welfare state beyond the role implied by earlier social philosophies is that there seemed to be no theoretical limit as to what was to count as a legitimate area for state intervention. The most important examples are health and education; for although they are welfare-enhancing to individuals there is, superficially at least, little about those services which makes them appropriate for public provision: their benefits are experienced by *private* individuals. Even if, following the reasoning of the new liberals, it is accepted that equality and social justice were intrinsic features of a welfare society, it does not follow at all that those imperatives necessitate the public, and compulsory, provision of health, education and so on, at zero price at the point of consumption.

There are some arguments (to be considered later) which

purport to show that such activities enhance the well-being of the public taken collectively rather than merely effect redistribution to the needy. If the latter were the justification, it is hardly satisfactory since redistribution through cash transfers is historically and theoretically a much more efficient method of achieving social justice than the collective delivery of particular services in kind. It could be maintained that there are other features of welfare philosophy that are relevant to the extension of the state into what might be thought private areas. The most common is that a welfare society requires feelings of solidarity that transcend the cash nexus of markets, however 'justly' they are organized: a system which depends on price and private property, even if it is structured on egalitarian grounds, contaminates those relationships which ought to be conducted on the basis of 'mutuality', or some form of social solidarity.

The contemporary welfare debate has its roots both in the historical development of ideas and in the evolution of social institutions. However, theories of welfare seem not to represent a movement towards agreement on the establishment of 'scientific' propositions about social improvement. The arguments are often replays of familiar debates, involving the same values, propositions and irresolvable disputes. Although there have been periods of apparent consensus, these are short-lived and are often thin veneers of ideological unity beneath which debate flourished. The most intractable of the welfare disputes is that between individualist and collectivist conceptions of well-being, and their respective policy implications. This is the major concern of the rest of this book. Although much of it is concerned with the analytical aspects of the problems that this artificial dichotomy has spawned, it should not be forgotten that they have an important historical dimension. The problems of welfare are recurring ones.

4

Liberal Political Economy and Welfare

I

Contemporary liberal welfare economics is more than a restatement of the social philosophy formulated by Adam Smith and taken forward, if in a somewhat perverted form, by the utilitarians of the nineteenth century. Its reformulation in the 1960s and 1970s has involved not just a more rigorous statement of the individualism of liberal philosophy but also a systematic defence of the market order against a welfare state that had become established both politically and intellectually. In liberal political economy we find an attenuated view of welfare based upon narrow, rigid and uncompromisingly individualistic principles of human nature. Such principles do not exclude axiomatically some of the public services we now associate with the welfare state but their inclusion depends upon certain stringent conditions being met. Most important of all, liberal political economy clings, somewhat desperately, to the idea of a *science* of welfare, i.e. the attempt is made to construct a theory of welfare without invoking statements about what is 'good' and 'bad' for individuals independently of their subjective choices.

It should be noted in what sense the word 'welfare' is being used in the context of liberal political economy: it is the private, incommunicable experiences of each individual taken separately, and indeed 'isolated' from the individual's community, that are the relevant criteria of well-being. Even though the doctrine does not preclude collective provision of (carefully specified) goods and services, the rationale for it lies in the claim that only in such a form can certain individual satisfaction be achieved. It is no accident, then, that the word 'efficiency' is often used as a synonym for welfare in liberal individualism, for this is defined precisely as the satisfaction of necessarily subjective desires. In the tradition of methodological individualism, it is maintained that there is no such thing as a collective social welfare function which is not logically reducible to statements about individuals.[1]

However, a major problem is that, although state action may improve on the market in certain circumstances in this efficiency sense, it is difficult to see how this can be made entirely consistent with a rigorous individualism. While it is true that a market is an admirable mechanism for revealing people's preferences for normal goods and services, in those areas where it is conceded that the exchange mechanism is inefficient, there is the problem of finding an alternative mechanism which is consistent with individualism. Voting is an obvious surrogate for the market but majoritarian procedures, even if they work perfectly, do involve the imposition of decisions on unwilling people.

The attempt to provide a 'science' of welfare derives from the Italian economist, Vilfredo Pareto (1848–1923).[2] The 'Pareto principle' says that we can legitimately speak of a welfare improvement when a change makes persons (at least one person) better-off without making any one person worse-off. A market exchange which affects nobody adversely is clearly a Pareto-improvement and is quite consistent with the subjectivism of liberal political economy. The Pareto principle rests upon three assumptions: that each individual is the best judge of their own welfare, that social welfare is exclusively a function of individual welfare and that if one individual's welfare increases, while no-one's is diminished, then 'social' welfare increases. These assumptions may be said to embody value judgements. They are obviously not observations of a behaviourist kind, and they rest on individualistic assumptions about well-being and satisfaction which are by no means uncontroversial. Yet, nevertheless, these value judgements are thought to be so minimal as to command general assent. It would be odd to deny that a change that benefited some without in any way harming anybody else was a welfare improvement. The main complaint concerns the paucity of the Pareto principle as a *welfare* judgement rather than its invalidity.

It should be clear that this approach to welfare is different from conventional utilitarianism, at least of the nineteenth-century

Benthamite variety. For that did suppose that an 'objective' welfare (utility) function could be summed from the preferences of individuals. This requires an interpersonal comparison of utilities and some way of measuring the relative impact alternative policies have on persons. In theory, Benthamite utilitarianism is a potentially radical welfare doctrine that does compare alternative 'end-states', i.e. patterns of social well-being. But this approach is obviously evaluative: it says that some states of affairs are 'better', more efficient, welfare-enhancing and so on even though known individuals may be harmed (however minutely) by their imposition. However, because utilitarianism is much stronger in its welfare implications, policies sanctioned by it are likely to be much more contestable.

Since the Pareto criteria explicitly forbid the interpersonal comparability and cardinal measurability of utilities and is concerned entirely with the subjective choices of individuals, its evaluative significance is strictly limited: states of affairs can only be described as 'better' or more efficient if everybody agrees. Of particular significance is the privileged position that the status quo occupies, especially the distribution of resources from which Pareto-improvements may be made. Thus any move from the status quo, however unequal the distribution of resources contained within it, which was vetoed by one person would not be a Pareto-improvement. It is not that the acceptance of the status quo by Paretian welfare economics implies approval of it: the point is that the theory's silence on an initial distribution indicates an attempt to remain within the confines of economic 'science' rather than to branch out into a more substantive ethical philosophy. It leads to the superficially bizarre position that, for example, repeal of the Corn Laws in 1846 was not strictly a Pareto-improvement because it harmed the interests of the landowners: despite the fact that international free trade is the 'optimal' policy by the tenets of abstract economic theory. The problems occur when theorists add phrases such as 'better', 'more efficient' or 'welfare-enhancing' to the outcomes of some social or economic system. Thus it is not always the case that Paretian welfare economics conforms to the tenets of substantive liberal political economy.[3]

None of this precludes the welfare economist from making some comment on the status quo: the description of those economic and social circumstances from which trading begins. Indeed, many

Paretian welfare economists do say that it is perfectly proper to recommend a substantial rearrangement of initial economic resources
and then to regard the outcomes of free exchange as perfectly
acceptable. However, the rationale for the initial rearrangement
must derive from evaluative concepts, e.g. social justice or equality,
that belong properly to the realm of ethics and social philosophy
rather than *wertfrei* economic theory. It may also be the result of
some *political* process, but unless the validity of a voting process is
unanimously accepted, its outcomes would be antithetical to the
strict tenets of Paretian individualism.

Furthermore, a comment on the nature of the 'self' or 'agent'
that is the object of Paretian welfare economics is highly pertinent
to this austere liberal political economy. This agent is simply the
atomized individual found in orthodox micro-economics whose
identity is established in terms of more or less immediate desires
rather than by membership of a politically organized community.
Therefore, whatever entitlements to resources that he or she has,
derive from individualistic exchange, from gifts and so on, and not
from his or her status as a citizen.

This does not exclude the possibility of a welfare state delivering
extra-market payments. They may very well be voted for in the
democratic process which is itself regarded as legitimate, but the
form of entitlement will obviously be different from those that flow
from, say, membership of a society with common values and shared
resources. Liberal political economy denies that there are such
common values; there are only individual desires.

This refusal to countenance the relevance of morality in the construction of a welfare theory has a further interesting implication,
for it seems to preclude the making of moral judgements about the
recipients of welfare; it was this 'moralism' which was a characteristic of nineteenth-century social thought. Individualistic welfare
theory would seem to encourage a scepticism towards the frequent
conservative claim that indiscriminate welfare encourages the for-
mation of an undesirable moral character. There are, of course,
many liberal objections to the welfare state but it is difficult to see
how this can be one of them since the liberal cosmology, with its
relentless subjectivism, excludes the possibility of there being objective moral standards to which we all ought to conform. The most
common Paretian justification for welfare lies in the claim that the
relief of the indigence actually increases the well-being of the

donor, since the existence of such deprivation is a kind of 'public bad' (see below).

Of more immediate concern are two questions about liberal political economy and welfare. The first concerns the major claim of liberal political economy since Smith: that an untrammelled market, based on private property and free exchange, does maximize welfare in the limited sense of satisfying individual desires. Is this true or are there welfare improvements (in the limited sense permitted by liberal economics) which can only come about through collective action? The second concerns the crucial question of distribution. Is an account of welfare even conceivable which does not tackle this problem directly? Overriding this latter question is the plausibility of the liberal individualist's justification of welfare outside the market.

II

Although the question of whether a free market maximizes social welfare has become a technical question of economic theory, it has a direct relevance to politics and the legitimate role of the state in social life. It is quintessentially a problem of equilibrium: an economy is in equilibrium when the actions of decentralized agents are so coordinated that all desires are satisfied, resources are not wasted, and the prices of all goods and services exactly reflect costs of production.[4] It is a fundamental claim of liberal political economy that a perfectly competitive equilibrium satisfies the Pareto-criterion of social welfare: that no charge can be made without making one person worse-off.

It should be noted that the ideal of a perfectly-competitive equilibrium has many welfare-enhancing features apart from the fact that it represents the satisfaction of individual desires. Leaving aside the important problem of inequality of initial resource endowments, the competitive market has many properties that are favourable to egalitarianism of a certain type. Prices of goods and services reflect marginal cost (the theoretical absence of monopoly means that no producer can reduce output and raise price because of exclusive ownership of a vital resource), and each factor of production (land, labour and capital) is paid just that sufficient income to ensure maximum productivity so that there are no entrepreneurial 'profits'. It is, indeed, no wonder that the original market socialists of the 1930s, notably Oskar Lange and Abba Lerner,[5] regarded the equilibrium model as a criterion for rational socialist production. They took exactly the same concept of man, i.e. the person was simply a self-interested maximizer of utility, as the orthodox liberal economists but argued that existing capitalist market systems failed to exploit the potential welfare possibilities of economic society. Most contemporary socialists now recognise that markets are not merely engines of profit but actually create the opportunities for maximizing everybody's welfare. The controversial question is about their limitations.[6]

It is not difficult to see that existing capitalist systems are deficient when set against the standards of pure equilibrium theory. The prevalence of monopoly and other market imperfections indicates that there are opportunities for the state to intervene so as to bring about welfare improvements for society as a whole. However, a strict interpretation of the Pareto principle would imply that monopolists should be compensated for the loss of their privileges existing in the status quo, a position too conservative for many liberal political economists. Equally plausible opportunities for the state to make welfare improvements on the market lie in the areas of externalities and public goods.[7] Externalities are normally harms (though they can be benefits) imposed on third parties and society at large by decentralized agents which for technical reasons cannot be priced by the market. Public goods are explained with the same logic: in the purest sense they are goods which are non-rival (the consumption by one or more persons does not reduce the amount available to others) and are non-excludable (once supplied, those who have not paid for them cannot be prevented from consuming them). The interesting point (to be considered below) is that many liberal economists try to justify some features of the redistributive welfare state by a version of the public good/externality argument, i.e. redistribution can make everyone better off and not merely the recipients.

Superficially, the description of the liberal theory of welfare seems to be firmly tilted towards *laissez-faire*, with the state limited to the correction of market failure and individual choice determining an efficient allocation of resources. However, market socialists and other theorists of market failure have managed to expand the area of the state so as to produce an un-liberal state on, ironically, *liberal* grounds. Once it is conceded that an equilibrium may not be reached spontaneously (through the exercise of Adam Smith's 'natural liberty') there are few theoretical limits to that desirable outcome being produced by artifice. Thus the modern capitalist economy is replete with anti-monopoly legislation, economic regulation and welfare institutions and policies, all of which have a plausible economic rationale.

In fact, the contemporary theory of liberalism does not describe the welfare properties of free markets in terms of their satisfying some equilibrium end-state of the perfect coordination of human actions. The most distinguished of contemporary liberal philosophers, F.A. von Hayek,[8] specifically precludes the justification of the market in terms of its maximization of some aggregate welfare function, least of all one that requires the adding and comparing of individual utilities. The argument here is as much epistemological as it is economic. The claim is that no central planner can ever know, in advance of the operation of a market process itself, just what properties an equilibrium end-state of product coordination would display. Economic knowledge, unlike the engineering types of knowledge contained in a physical system, is dispersed across all the human actors in an economic process. Furthermore, such knowledge is of a fleeting, ephemeral kind that cannot be captured in 'plans' or artificial schemes of improvement.

One nice example, to illustrate the contrast between equilibrium welfare economics and the political economy of liberalism, is the problem of monopoly. It is quite possible that a 'natural' monopoly, i.e. single supplier of a wanted good, could emerge from an unhampered market. The supplier, by fixing the price above marginal cost, would then earn a monopoly 'rent' or abnormal profit. In the economist's sense, welfare or efficiency could be increased by taxing away the profit, nationalizing the activity or by some other method of ensuring that an equilibrium price is charged. However, many liberal political economists deny that such intervention is necessarily welfare-enhancing.[9]

This scepticism is maintained for a number of reasons. First, it is argued that the occurrence of genuine natural monopolies is rather rare: most examples are, in fact, the product of some special state privilege. Secondly, when they do occur, it is claimed that the prospect of potential competition from new entrants goes some way towards reducing the excess profits of the monopolist. Thus, an essential feature of government policy must be the maintenance of an open and competitive market. Thirdly, it is held that the prospect of excess profits may be the only way of encouraging individuals into risky activities. Fourthly, and most important, is the point that if a government were to maximize welfare in the economist's sense, how could it *know* what the appropriate price would be in the absence of a market? Since the market itself is the most appropriate mechanism for the expression of individual choice, and since equilibrium welfare economics does identify well-being in terms of individual subjective experiences, the attenuation of that mechanism would mean the removal of essential sources of information about choices. It is true that voting is itself an expression of individual choice, and that liberal individuals recognise its necessity in some welfare areas, but it is hardly likely to be so in the area of monopoly and other market imperfections.

If the welfare properties of the market are not to be found by reference to some imaginary equilibrium, what then are its virtues? The key to this is contained in Adam Smith's phrase, 'natural liberty', which simply refers to the freedom of individuals to make the best use of that decentralized knowledge that is available to them in a complex society. The welfare criterion within this is that of *indirect* utility, i.e. the well-being of a community is the accidental product of individual striving rather than the deliberate creation of a perfectly coordinated set of economic arrangements. In the absence of the centralized knowledge that would be required to effect such plans, it is claimed that the market process itself, despite its imperfections, is constantly correcting allocational errors and hence nudging the system towards an equilibrium. It is an equilibrium which, however, is likely to be disrupted by changes in the data that confront individual transactors. Thus although entrepreneurial 'profit', and hence theoretically alterable inequality, has to exist to power the system, this is likely to be precarious, and vulnerable to the competitive process itself.[10]

Although such an analysis claims to be positivist in the sense that it purports to describe objectively how market systems are to be understood irrespective of their moral worth, it contains implicitly at least two welfare judgements which are of crucial importance to the explication of the liberal political economy value systems and the theory of the welfare state. The first is the stress on the market as an arena in which individual autonomy is exercised. If autonomous action is described as purposive action that emanates from human agents who are not subject to extraneous forces of a causal kind, then free exchange between individuals is said to realize this more effectively than known alternative forms of social organization. If it is true that a human society is characterized by radical uncertainty and unpredictability then experimentation and innovation can only come from the actions of decentralized individuals. All market theorists, from Adam Smith to the present day, dispute the claim, made for example by Hobhouse and the 'New Liberals', that the market is itself a causal force that impoverishes individuals and renders them incapable of autonomous action.

From this emphasis on autonomy and self-determination it follows that, although self-interest is a crucial mechanism for the efficient allocation of resources according to individual preferences, the features of the market are not exhausted by egoistic action. The market system entails liberty and this can be exercised in directions which are the product of each person's autonomous will. This enabling feature of the market is essential for the explanation of the historical fact that welfare systems, mutual aid and the like, have developed outside the state. Liberal political economists do not deny that there may be a justification for state welfare but would claim that, in the form in which it is conventionally delivered, it represents a loss of autonomy: it is indeed their major criticism of the post-war welfare state.

The second welfare judgement implicit in liberal political economy concerns the results of market processes. For although liberal political economy does not claim that the justification for markets lies in their meeting the standards set by some abstract aggregate welfare function, much of the argument is consequentialist in that the exchange system is said to be 'better', in a utilitarian sense, at enhancing well-being, including that of the poorest. Even Hayek, who lays great stress on the unknowability and unpredictability of human action, and uses that argument against governments' pursuing 'optimal' welfare policies, has a vague conception of a desirable welfare policy. An economic policy is optimal, he claims, if it is directed towards 'increasing the chances of any member of society taken at random of having a high income'.[11] Although this is not an attempt to appraise markets for their welfare-enhancing properties in any quantitative sense, it is not quite the same as an evaluation of the market in terms of its contribution to individual autonomy. The admission of some collectivist

criterion of welfare seems unavoidable even in the most individualistic of doctrines.

The point here is that liberal political economy does very much
depend for its persuasiveness on some sort of aggregative criterion:
it is a rare individualist who maintains a complete silence about its
outcomes and who limits themself to an appraisal of the rules and
procedures (and the rights that they embody) of various social and
economic systems. As Amartya Sen has remarked: 'It is hard to
imagine that the value of the market can be divorced from the value
of its results and achievements.'[12] Few would deny that the liberal
market economy has historically allocated resources efficiently, at
least in comparison to the known alternatives, and therefore, in the
narrow economic sense, it has enhanced welfare.

III

It is an orthodoxy of market philosophy that there are some subjective wants that cannot be satisfied by the exchange process.
Although many liberals would deny that the invocation of an hypothetical equilibrium is a satisfactory way of justifying state intervention, they would claim that such measures are legitimate. The
general rubric is the theory of public goods and externalities. The
claim that such things as defence, law and order, clean air and so on,
have to be provided collectively because no one person has any
incentive to provide them is a familiar one; what is less familiar is
the argument that welfare and the alleviation of deprivation can be
similarly provided: that welfare is a public good, the state provision
of which can be justified on the very same individualistic and subjectivist grounds that underpin the collective provision of the more
conventional public goods, such as defence and clean air.

In a famous passage Milton Friedman writes:

> I am distressed by the sight of poverty; I am benefitted by its allevia-
> tion; the benefits of other people's charity therefore partly accrue to
> me. To put it differently we might all of us be willing to contribute to
> the relief of poverty, provided everyone else did.[13]

The claim being made here is that the relief of deprivation is a
genuine public good that everyone desires but which will not be
provided voluntarily because of the incentive structure that faces
individuals. The contribution that each person would make to the

relief of indigence is so infinitesimally small that it would not be worthwhile making it. If it were to be significant, it would require the cooperation of many individuals who, given the behavioural assumptions common to all liberal individualist thought, would be likely to defect from any voluntary agreement. Thus, although the provision of welfare does depend upon individual altruistic prefer- ences, the private market is technically inefficient at registering these. It is not that welfare is justified on paternalist grounds, or that the redistribution it entails is intrinsically 'right' or socially just, but that its compulsory provision benefits everybody, including the preferences of the donors. It has been correctly, and paradoxically, called a kind of 'voluntary compulsion'.

Leaving aside for the moment the fundamental question of whether or not welfare is a genuine public good, the formulation above has a number of implications. Given that this justification of state welfare is not paternalist and that it claims to make its exist- ence compatible with liberty, it would seem to follow, and it is cer- tainly an inference which Friedman makes, that welfare ought to be distributed in cash and not tied to any particular pattern of con- sumption. It also seems that the delivery of welfare should not be accompanied by any reciprocal obligations on the part of its recip- ients: it is their distress that has to be alleviated not their moral con- dition. In this it is consistent with the relentless subjectivism of liberalism, and not compatible with certain nineteenth-century welfare theories that tried to connect the relief of indigence with the cultivation of a certain moral character. This form of welfare would also seem to gel readily with the liberal idea of a society as a loosely coordinating set of anonymous traders, identified by the universal characteristics of self-interest, rather than by their membership of a particular community: a notion of individuality which is as alien to conservative thought as it is to socialism.

Although this liberal argument does hold that the relief of indi- gence is a public good, it still permits individualist critics of the welfare state to maintain that the conventional array of services provided by contemporary welfare states – health, education, pen- sions, and so on – are in fact private goods, since they are consumed in discrete amounts by identifiable individuals, and therefore could be supplied more efficiently by the market. When the public good of welfare is delivered in this form, it offends liberal, subjectivist principles since the state (and compulsory) provision of particular services implies paternalism; it suggests that individuals are incapable of making the right or 'rational' choices. John Stuart Mill, for example, although by no means opposed to redistribution, was hostile to the idea of a uniform and compulsory system of education precisely because it would endanger that pluralism and respect for individual choice that characterizes a liberal society.

However, it has not proved impossible for writers to argue that 'efficiency' could be maximized by the state delivery of particular welfare services: it has been maintained that everybody or 'society' would be better off if there were collectivized unemployment insurance, education, pensions, healthcare, and so on. It is argued that these activities are legitimate apart from any distributive criteria that may be used to validate the state's role. Although such defences would not require that private provision of such services be forbidden, they do entail that individuals be compelled to participate in collective schemes.

One familiar rationale is that a technically efficient allocation of resources, one that perfectly matched the provision of services with people's subjective choices, requires that individuals be fully-informed rational-agents: but if individuals are ignorant of relevant facts, then producers of a vital service may be able to extract 'rents' from helpless consumers in virtue of their monopoly of knowledge. Government intervention here could surely make the market more efficient? The existence of a nationalized health system is often justified in precisely this way.

Another efficiency argument for some state involvement in the supply of what might be thought to be private welfare goods derives from the alleged short-sightedness of individuals. For example, individuals may have too high time preferences, i.e. they discount the future at too high a rate for an orderly organization of economy and society. Thus compulsory old-age pensions contributions are justified because those individuals who value the present too much will not save for their retirement and hence leave government a welfare problem in the form of many aged and indigent people. Since it is unlikely that a government will simply let them take the consequences of their improvidence it will therefore provide them with welfare. However, this will in fact encourage people to be improvident, thus generating 'moral hazard' on a massive scale.[14]

Nevertheless, leaving aside the question as to whether such government actions are responses to genuine market failure, which can be doubted, it is surely the case that the theory which underlies them embraces significant modifications of the original liberal individualist explanation of a welfare improvement. The most important of these is the serious attenuation of the subjectivist principle that each person is the best judge of their own interest. This must be so in relation to compulsory national insurance for, say, healthcare and pensions. No doubt a case can be made for this but it is difficult to avoid the conclusion that it is a paternalist one. Such arguments are common in welfare theory and are not to be rejected automatically. Indeed, nineteenth-century welfare policies and institutions, such as the Poor Law, had strong paternalist overtones and utilitarianism, at least in its public policy manifestations, does not exclude it. In fact, the absence of paternalism in pure liberal individualism makes a crucially important distinction between this doctrine and almost all other welfare philosophies.

Furthermore, the argument that efficiency improvements can be made by state action because of the information problems associated with private action in free markets depends upon a subtle misrepresentation of the liberal individualist position. It is certainly true that if there is to be an efficient allocation of resources in economic society (and hence a situation of maximum possible welfare), it has to be assumed that individual buyers and sellers are fully informed of all relevant facts and alternative courses of action. However, the absence of this informational utopia does not entail that the liberal case for the market is automatically invalidated. This would be to confuse market liberalism with 'equilibrium' political economy.[15] As we have seen, in the liberal case for markets in ordinary goods and services, the value of the exchange process lies *not* in its achievement of a perfect coordination of actions but in the opportunities it gives for individuals to exploit that dispersed knowledge which all complex societies display. There is no reason why the familiar welfare goods are necessarily different. Thus, even though individuals are usually ignorant about the technicalities of healthcare, it cannot be assumed that competition between suppliers would be less 'efficient' than the authoritative determination by political authorities. Furthermore, just how much people want to spend on health is itself a subjective phenomenon (healthcare is after all a scarce good which is in competition with other wanted goods) and, if we wish to keep within the liberal individualist framework, we cannot assume that the state, even, or perhaps especially, with a democratic voting system, is any better than the market in revealing people's preferences for it.

It is not difficult to see how modern welfare economists have managed to validate a wider extension of state activity in the welfare field than is permitted by classical liberalism under the superficially anodyne rubric of market failure, and without resort to the ethically more controversial claims of overt distributive criteria, such as equality and social justice. Indeed, contemporary welfare economists may be seen as twentieth-century representatives of Edwin Chadwick in that they start from a commitment to individualism and the market's allocative mechanisms, yet, by a series of discrete steps in health, education, pensions, housing and so on, generate a total welfare system which seems remote from those original liberal foundations. It is, however, difficult to see how any collective welfare judgement, i.e. for a society as a whole, can be derived from individual values, characterized as they are in complex societies by diversity and incommensurability. What is even more disputable is the claim that the collective provision of such welfare is consistent with liberty (although it may have some other ethical rationale).

IV

Although it is difficult to extend the liberal concept of welfare to the provision of what are in effect private goods, there is still the question of whether a minimal role for welfare, in the sense of the relief of indigence, is itself compatible with liberal individualism. To many liberals, including the aforementioned *laissez-faire* economist Milton Friedman, it seemed obvious that, although charitable activity is desirable, this alone would not be sufficient to satisfy individuals' altruistic preferences because of the public-good problem. To the liberal individualist, the state is not acting paternalistically here because it would be giving effect to the desires of both the donors and recipients of welfare: surely a genuine welfare improvement?

However, this proposition is by no means accepted by all liberal theorists. For one thing, it is difficult to see how there could be any charitable activity at all if there is such a public-good trap: if my contribution makes little or no difference to the supply of welfare, and if my altruistic preferences are satisfied by the contributions of others, then where is the incentive to provide for welfare voluntarily? Yet, clearly there is an abundance of voluntary activity in Western societies. Indeed, there is good empirical evidence that charitable donations tend to rise as incomes rise, although at a disproportionate rate.[16] Furthermore, there is an empirical connection between declining tax burdens and an increase in philanthropy.

However, it is just as plausible to suppose that individuals give to charity out of a sense of moral duty, *irrespective of what other people are doing*, rather than expressing some altruistic preference.[17] If people donate for moral reasons, then there is no public-good problem because the binding nature of the duty holds for each individual quite apart from the total amount of welfare supplied. It does not, of course, at all follow from the existence of a moral duty in a community that there would be sufficient income to finance today's welfare state, although it might well be sufficient to relieve obvious indigence. It is also the case that the absence of the contemporary welfare state would mean that taxes were lower and, presumably, the motivation to fulfil a moral duty that much higher. It is surely plausible to suppose that many people now regard their moral duties as being fulfilled precisely because there already exists a wide range of tax-financed welfare services.

As Robert Sugden[18] argues, in an abstract but penetrating critique of the public-good theory of welfare, it is most unlikely that there exists a sufficiently widespread altruistic sentiment to justify the prevailing structure of welfare services. The altruist is not concerned directly about his own contribution to a charity but only about his private consumption and the total income of the charity. Since, for the altruist, it does not matter who donates, because the charitable activity benefits anyway, the public-good theory has the odd and implausible implication that a person would actually give larger proportions of increases in their own income if they knew that the charity's income was falling from other sources. It is only the public-good trap that prevents such donations – hence the rationale of the welfare state. As Sugden notes,[19] there is a curious parallel between *laissez-faire* classical liberals, who justify a paradoxically, 'compulsory voluntaristic' system of welfare on the grounds of an alleged altruistic impulse, and more collectivist social theorists who invoke a similar 'caring' hypothesis to demonstrate the ultimate morality of state welfare.

It is not, then, implausible to suppose that people's sense of moral duty is sufficient to generate some voluntary provision for the relief of indigence irrespective of their perception of the total income of a charity. Although it is unlikely that such voluntarism would be sufficient to generate the range and extent of existing welfare states this is, in fact, immaterial. The prevailing liberal public-good justification for welfare does not do this either. For one thing, it is difficult to maintain that the public provision of essentially private goods is justifiable on efficiency grounds and for another, its typical compulsory components, for example in social insurance and pensions, do involve losses in liberty. The idea of 'voluntary compulsion' that underlies the public-good justification for welfare is a misnomer that conceals a serious conflict of ethical values. Whether a fully-fledged welfare system can be reconciled with the liberal tradition remains an open question.

V

As has been suggested earlier, even if it is conceded that liberal political economy explains how markets maximize both efficiency and freedom of choice, which are both crucially important welfare-enhancing properties, the doctrine itself is normally silent on the distribution of property rights from which Pareto-improvements can be made. The trouble is that in its endeavour to maintain a 'science' of welfare, or at least a doctrine with the minimal of ethical postulates, it disables itself from comment on those distributive questions which are the very stuff of the welfare debate. Thus, although it can be persuasively argued that a voluntary exchange between two (or more) parties constitutes a welfare improvement because it would meet with (almost) unanimous approval, the same could not be said about the respective economic positions of the traders, i.e. their property holdings. These are as likely to be the result of luck (for example, inheritance) as they are of effort (labour exchange). To make a judgement about this, however, would be to depart from the original minimalist values implicit in liberal theory. Indeed, it is the lack of agreement in complex, industrial societies on the ethical criteria appropriate for such distributive questions that reinforces the individualist's somewhat theatrical silence on this issue. Questions of distribution are regarded as not amenable to rational enquiry: all welfare is a mass of conflicting opinions and incommensurable values. Whatever justifications liberal individualists offer for original property titles, they have little to do with social welfare. Most, in fact, are either conservative–utilitarian acceptances of the status quo or natural rights and entitlement theories derived from John Locke.

The difficulty, of course, in liberal welfare theory is that the distribution of property titles can have an effect on the outcomes of a market process and hence lend a certain plausibility to the claim that markets can, in effect, be coercive, even though their mechanisms are defined in terms of voluntarism and agreement. Although this proposition will be considered in more detail in Chapter 5, a mention of one spectacular example of the problem is a useful introduction to the general issue.

Amartya Sen, in his work on famine in India,[20] has shown how catastrophes can occur, and in fact, have occurred through the peaceful operation of market processes in which rights are not violated and lawful processes honoured. He cites cases where, with an overall sufficiency of food supplies, mass and avoidable starvation occurred because the market failed to allocate resources to those in obvious need. It was not then a *natural* catastrophe for which the market could not be 'blamed' but in a sense an 'artificial' one brought about by the distribution of property rights in combination with an exchange system that is indifferent to human welfare.

Such phenomena may be remote from the welfare problems that concern complex, Western industrial societies. Indeed, their frequency may be doubted and, certainly, we cannot assume a priori that collective measures would be more effective in averting such calamities. The evidence of famines in societies characterized by the elimination of market systems is equally, if not more, compelling.[21] Nevertheless, Sen does generalize his argument by claiming that, in the market economies of the West, if people do not go begging for food it is only because of the 'social security system that the state has offered'.[22] This is a rather strong claim: few collectivist theorists would maintain that in the West some people would be threatened with actual starvation in an untrammelled market system; rather, it is argued that they would be deprived of that share in prosperity which a non-individualist social welfare theory would validate.

The real problem for liberal political theory is to construct a welfare philosophy which maintains the non-coercive feature of individualism without exposing itself to the kind of criticism made by Sen. There really are only two possibilities: either the political system should be so designed that it accurately reflects the sentiments that individuals do have for the relief of indigence, or those possibilities for purely voluntary arrangements, which have existed throughout history, should be given more attention. Perhaps some combination of the two would constitute a desirable welfare policy.

It has already been suggested that it is unlikely that there exists an altruistic sentiment widespread enough to validate the existing welfare system along the lines of the public-good argument. But this begs the question of the morality and efficiency of the existing welfare system. However, some liberals would still maintain that there is a public-good element in welfare, and therefore that this is consistent with subjectivism if it is supplied as a result of people's *political* choices through the voting system. But they would go on to argue that the existing simple majority-rule systems of Western democracies are inefficient at expressing the welfare sentiment, i.e. they allow coalitions of interests to exploit the system for the benefit of minorities not in need. Indeed, the welfare state, because it supplies many goods and services in kind, has developed (perhaps accidentally) as a complex structure of private interests, with much evidence of redistribution *away* from the lower-income groups to middle-income groups (see Chapter 6). If there is a welfare sentiment which can only be expressed through public institutions, as many liberal individualists maintain, then one solution to the problem would be in the direction of removing the inefficiencies of the political system rather than concentrating exclusively on 'market failure' and intrinsically desirable policies.

The Critique of Individualism and the Ethics of Welfare

I

The broad liberal tradition discussed in Chapter 4 is remarkable for its attempt to construct a welfare theory that depends only to a limited extent on ethics. Although there is a general assumption that, in a utilitarian sense, the efficiency properties of a competitive market tend to lead to an allocation of resources from which everybody, including the worst-off, gains, the rationale for this is as much 'scientific' as it is ethical. The only moral value that is relevant to this would appear to be *freedom* (apart from the formal rules of justice that are essential to the working of an exchange system); but even this concept is understood in the traditional negative sense in which a person's liberty is a function of the absence of (alterable) coercive laws. It is the strait-jacket imposed by the prohibition on interpersonal comparisons of individual utilities (which a science of welfare requires) that rules out an ethics of redistribution. The rationale for extra-market payments to the needy depends on the existence of altruistic sentiments on a community. In liberal political economy, a welfare society is defined by the combination of market efficiency which will aid the least advantaged (the much-vaunted 'trickle-down' effect) and benevolence. In no way can the market be said to *cause* indigence.

One important, and often underestimated reason for the liberal political economist's objection to the argument that the distribution of resources determined by the market ought to be disturbed by moral principles external to it, is that, apart from the misallocative effects the implementation of these will have, there is so little agreement on such redistributive criteria. For example, although 'needs' may appear to be objective, beyond a certain minimum level of resources required for survival, a standard that is surely easily met in contemporary Western societies, there is nothing more than a welter of conflicting wants, all demanding satisfaction from necessarily limited resources. Social justice, a seductive ideal that commends the substitution of genuine moral criteria, such as desert and effort, for the amoral decisions of the labour market in the determination of income, is similarly plagued with irresolvable conflict. In the absence of a genuine hierarchy of values, the processing of welfare demands through the democratic system produces random distributions of resources which are as much a reflection of political power as they are of ethical principle.

However, the liberal individualist's theory of welfare is not exhausted by a description of the ethics and efficiency of the market. In the literature of social welfare, a dichotomy between the market and the state is frequently posited, and it is maintained that the cold mechanisms of the market, because they are powered by self-interest, cannot be sensitive to welfare 'needs' precisely because these are not translatable into prices; or, more accurately, those in need lack the resources to pay the prices set by the market.

This dichotomy is misleading on two grounds. First, it cannot be assumed a priori that the state is sensitive to those needs (a point to be considered later). Secondly, it elides the possibility of there being a realm of human action that is neither political nor economic (in the narrow sense). Thus, the correct dichotomy should be between freedom and coercion. Also, freedom is not limited to market exchanges, for the absence of coercion increases the opportunities for individuals to engage in a variety of forms of social organization. It it is not meant simply that individuals could purchase for themselves the typical welfare goods, pensions, health, social insurance and so benefit from this 'privatization', for even if it were accompanied by some redistributive measures to counter an unacceptable inequality of access to resources, it would still link freedom to experiences of market prices. It is possible, however, for freedom to be exercised outside this nexus and be conducive to shared welfare ideals. Reference can be made here to 'mutual aid' organizations[1] or 'friendly societies', in which individuals in small groups, through voluntary action, cater for the welfare of their members. It is here that allegedly non-market criteria of 'need' can operate yet be outside the framework of formal 'definitions' of need set by the state. The functions of early trade unions included activity of this kind, immigrants form similar associations, and 'anarchist' writers[2] frequently point to these as examples of social phenomena that escape the conceptual exclusiveness of market and state. Such organizations are held together by a complex network of reciprocal obligations. Historically, these associations have been largely taken over by the state; the result of this was that social welfare arrangements tended to become either 'public' and organized by the state or 'private' and determined by price.

Yet the misleading dichotomy between market and state has dominated the ethics of welfare since the New Liberalism of the early part of this century and it is this that has led to a further confusion between competition and cooperation. This latter contrast has led to the description of the market as uncooperative, a game from which there are only winners and losers rather than exchange from which there are mutual benefits. It was no doubt an attitude that was encouraged by Herbert Spencer. Hence Richard Titmuss wrote that: 'Capitalism is a biological failure: it is promoting the extinction of society.'[3] Although most collectivist welfare theorists (including Titmuss himself) would not reject the market *per se*, they do maintain that it is the *cause* of those economic misfortunes that render some people in need of welfare.

It is important to be clear what is meant by 'causality' here. It is assumed that the welfare theorist would not claim that the market system caused those natural infirmities that render, from birth, certain people incapable of normal participation in society, although, presumably the responses different economic systems make to genetic catastrophe is subject to moral criticism. The argument is surely that so far from markets improving well-being, their remorseless allocative processes create 'innocent' victims of (economically) necessary change. J.S. Schumpeter's famous description of the 'gales of creative destruction' brought about by individualistic entrepreneurship fails to mention the casualties that follow in their wake. Thus, whereas the classical liberal notion of causality relates to responsibility for action (hence the reluctance to entertain easily obtainable welfare because it is likely to produce irresponsible and improvident behaviour), the social welfare theorist understands causality as running in the opposite direction. Some writers would go further and claim that the mere fact of 'vulnerability' is itself sufficient to justify a claim on resources, irrespective of any causal mechanisms that could be said to be operative.[4]

Since market relationships are competitive, so the theory goes, they must also be divisive, sundering those communal links between individuals which are required to cope with those calamities to which we are all vulnerable. The important general principle here is 'solidarity': it means that a society's welfare is not reducible to individual experiences of well-being to which he or she is entitled to by his or her own efforts and contributions, but consists of a complex amalgam of rational and communal sentiments. It might even be said, although in a language not favoured by social welfare theorists, that individuals by living in society in fact receive economic 'rent', i.e. the difference between the income they would receive outside society and that which they actually get because of the existence of a social cooperation which they do not directly create. Thus welfare is really a form of 'compensation' drawn from collective resources.

The effect of the penetration of society by the market principle is to dissolve these necessary social bonds. The most eloquent defence of this position is to be found in Titmuss's *The Gift Relationship*,[5] a book which not only contains a technical comparison of the supply of blood by price and by donation, but also explains the ethics that underlie the welfare state principle. The point is that if this, the most sacred commodity of all, is commercialized, then everything will be contaminated by price so that there are no moral bonds at all. The ethical feature of blood donation is that it is, in essence, a gift to a stranger; it is given irrespective of entitlements, *reciprocal* obligations (of which there are none), prices and all of the other concepts of individualistic ethics and economics. Titmuss writes that:

> In not asking for or expecting any payment of money those donors signified their belief in the willingness of other men to act altruistically in the future, and to combine together to make a gift freely should they have a need for it. By expressing confidence in the behaviour of future unknown strangers they were thus denying the Hobbesian thesis that men are devoid of any instinctive moral sense.[6]

Although there may be something to the argument that the marketing of certain activities may cause a decline in altruistic motives (for example, the knowledge that blood is priced may adversely affect the desire to donate[7]) the general argument that the welfare state is justifiable on altruistic principles is impossible to sustain. The transfers that it entails are obviously coerced and, indeed, non-selfish behaviour is much more likely to occur in the context of reciprocal obligations (the moral phenomena the relevance of which Titmuss denies) than between strangers. It seems fanciful to suppose that the very existence of welfare institutions and policies will somehow promote that spirit of solidarity and altruism which will eventually make the coercive elements in those arrangements redundant. It would be to claim that those features of human action identified by classical economists are not universal but dependent upon particular circumstances (there is a parallel here with early advocates of public ownership who naively believed that the absence of 'profit' in those enterprises would encourage more cooperative attitudes in employees). However, the evidence of behavioural adaptation to welfare policies, i.e. adjusting action to take full (and often 'unfair') advantage of the benefits they offer, is too strong a feature of contemporary societies (see Chapter 6) to make the argument at all plausible.

However, this does not dispose of the claim that untrammelled markets cause welfare problems, that the pursuit of 'efficiency' creates avoidable suffering. In an important sense, any progressive economic system will render certain occupations obsolete and particular communities vulnerable to the side-effects of the change. The market system is no more or less ethical than any other system in this respect. It cannot be assumed a priori that the emergence and expansion of the welfare state in the twentieth century is explicable entirely as a rational response to the alleged ravages upon communities brought about by the market.

As critics of nineteenth-century capitalism were assiduous in pointing out, it was the unpredictability of economic change that made the liberal notion of individual responsibility for action irrelevant. It was the existence of this phenomenon that led to the growth of *social* insurance, first in Germany and later in Britain. However, this reasoning is less persuasive in relation to the structure of contemporary welfare states.The point is that social insurance is basically a liberal notion (although the fact that it is

compulsory does mark a departure from strict individualistic principles) since it links, in theory at least, benefits to contributions and
therefore eliminates means-testing. It was greatly admired by
Beveridge for this reason. He once said that: 'Management of
one's income is an essential element of a citizen's freedom.'[8] If this
is a surrogate for a market principle then it is hard to see how a
free exchange system causes (in the strong sense of the word) distress. It would certainly not explain the curious phenomenon,
observable in the UK, USA and elsewhere, of increasing numbers
of people becoming dependent on some form of state assistance as
economic prosperity increases. This is not to deny the problem of
the 'uninsurable' (those born with genetic handicaps); however,
the bulk of the welfare state's activity is not aimed at this minority.

It is equally plausible that some of the typical policies and institutions of the welfare state themselves have a tendency to exacerbate the problem they are designed to solve, a phenomenon that is
itself explicable by causal laws. A spectacular example is the tendency of the numbers of homeless to rise in the UK, despite a stag-
nant or declining population and an excess of housing units. The
number of homeless is taken by prominent welfare theorists,
Raymond Plant and Kenneth Hoover,[9] as evidence of the market
causing welfare problems: it fails to provide housing to those in
demonstrable need. The reason why the market does not allocate
housing to those in need can surely be explained by a series of discrete government interventions throughout the century which have
summed to a complex web of inefficiencies.[10] The major interventions are rent control and aid to owner-occupiers. Placing a ceiling
on rents simply reduces the incentives for landlords to let property
(the income received from controlled rents may not even cover
essential maintenance) and the traditional subsidy to owner-occupiers, tax relief on mortgages, encourages people to overinvest in
housing. This latter intervention has the further effect of raising the
price of housing, thus inducing landlords to sell into the owner-
occupied sector property that was previously let. Furthermore,
security of tenure and low rents in the public sector encourage
people to stay in these properties irrespective of 'objective' need.
Thus, the seemingly inexorable rise in homelessness is much more
to do with the perverse effect of political action rather than some
causal mechanism operating in the market process.

If it is true that similar perverse effects are operative elsewhere in state welfare, it is quite likely that this phenomenon occurs because they are 'universally' available irrespective of objective need. In Titmuss's social philosophy universalism, in principle, has the ethical advantage of promoting social solidarity over the alleged divisiveness of the individualistic market system. Yet will not the perverse effects of universalist systems reproduce that same divisiveness in the public sphere?

II

Nevertheless, the existence of perverse effects does not undermine the ethical case for state welfare; they may be seen as technical rather than moral problems which carefully designed schemes could eliminate or at least reduce in intensity. There are other moral cases for welfare which do not rest on the somewhat implausible ground of altruism and which have developed in recent years as a response to some potent criticisms of welfare from the radical right.

The sophisticated moral justifications for state welfare are more individualistic than communal and exploit the traditional liberal concepts of freedom and rights. In fact, they perhaps represent the completion of that tradition rather than a rejection of it: those rules and procedures that enable individuals to pursue their subjectively-determined ends are inadequate if they fail to pay attention to those basic objective needs which make a meaningful life possible. Such theories still depend to some extent on the argument that the market causes distress. If it does so, it undermines that notion of individual autonomy which is said to be integral to it. A welfare theorist of this type would not deny that some deprivation does occur, such as genetic misfortune, which has nothing to do with the exchange process, but would maintain that insofar as the market's ethics impose no obligation to relieve such suffering, this is inconsistent with the liberal's belief in the equal autonomy of each individual (a position which does not necessarily invalidate the inequalities that result from the ways in which people make use of their equal autonomy). In effect, to refrain from aiding a person in deprivation, where such action is not excessively costly, is the moral equivalent of *harming* that person.

Thus the provision of welfare is not simply benevolence or part of a supererogatory morality (one concerned with actions which are morally praiseworthy but not strictly enforceable) but is a compelling duty. It is to be nicely contrasted with that altruism which underlies Titmuss's ethics: this latter, somewhat implausibly, locates the commitment to welfare in the context of something other than a network of enforceable obligations.

The theory is embedded in the notion of the autonomy of the person. A person who was formally free in the sense of not being restricted by coercive laws, would not be genuinely free if their choices did not emanate from their autonomous will. Thus, someone faced with the prospect of destitution or low wages may technically choose the latter but, in the circumstances, it is as if their actions were dictated by physical threat – they are caused. The liberal individualist believes that freedom is limited only by the intentional actions of human agents, and on this view, freedom cannot be limited by impersonal social forces since these cannot be directly reducible to observable individuals. However, Albert Weale claims that certain material conditions 'must necessarily hold for individuals to carry out a wide range of projects'.[11] Notice that this is not quite a theory of positive liberty, which would identify free action with rational action, but a theory that claims to be consistent with liberal subjectivism and pluralism. Weale argues that 'ultimately persons are the best judges of their own welfare'.[12] It is not that people make the 'wrong' choices but that in the absence of welfare some people's choices are arbitrarily narrowed. If liberalism requires the condition of equal autonomy for individuals and markets fail to provide it, then government action, paradoxically, is required to sustain the liberal social order.

In a not dissimilar way, Raymond Plant argues that the whole concept of agency, which the liberal tradition adheres to, is meaningless unless accompanied by a specification, in principle at least, of the conditions under which genuine moral choices can be made. He writes that: 'Basic needs have to be satisfied to do anything at all.'[13] Pluralism requires that individuals are able to carry out particular plans and projects and to make moral choices. What makes needs objective, as opposed to ephemeral, subjective wants, is that they are necessary means to the achievement of moral autonomy. Further, whereas wants cannot form the basis of a strict claim on others, needs can. The distinction between needs and wants turns upon the character of the ends to which they are related; the former are connected with the pursuit of the moral life itself while the latter are identified with the satisfaction of more or less immediate and transient desires. What makes need-satisfaction of overriding importance is that the failure to provide for it is morally equivalent to harming someone. The argument is that, with the obvious caveat that the agent charged with the responsibility of honouring such an obligation must be capable of so doing, to refrain from welfare-enhancing action because it is a supererogatory duty rather than a strict moral obligation is to cause that person's suffering.

Put this way the argument is plausible, even convincing. It makes sense to say 'X would not have died but for Y's wilful refusal to save him'. Y's inaction is wilful and causally responsible for X's death because the action required to save X can be performed at little or no cost to Y. It is difficult to conceive of moral codes that do not recognize such an obligation, and in some jurisdictions it is legally enforceable. It is also perfectly consonant with an ethic of reciprocity which imposes a universal obligation to relieve suffering precisely because *any* person might on some unknown occasion find himself in similar need.

Nevertheless, it is far too thin a reed on which to found a welfare state. The reason is that when the obligation is put in this form it applies to *any* moral agent. Indeed, historically, local communities and other associations smaller than the state, and private individuals, have recognized it. However, the activities of the welfare state involve significant redistribution and very clear choices between courses of action which are far from costless. Even the obligation to keep someone alive is not unambiguously compelling since improvements in medical technology make it possible to keep many people alive who would have died in earlier times. Doctors in the National Health Service have to 'ration' such technology and often they decide on crude utilitarian criteria, such as the potential earning power of the patients.

The caveat that obligations hold only so long as the cost of acting are low, limits the applicability of the argument that morality itself enjoins some welfare to a depressingly small number of cases. Furthermore, couched in this way, it is a universal principle; *everyone* is owed the obligation in the terms so described, yet the typical welfare problems, as opposed to 'life-saving' problems, are about entitlements and claims to resources in particular communities. It is doubtful that these very general moral considerations are all that relevant to the welfare issues of those communities.

III

Even if it is difficult to justify the welfare state from the ultimate principles of human agency, and the morality that pertains to it, some welfare philosophers still wish to formulate it in rights term – although the rights to such things as education, health, pensions and so on, are presumably claims against particular communities rather than possessed by all individuals.

However, it should be stressed that not all philosophers of welfare make a recourse to rights. Titmuss,[14] for example, was highly suspicious of a rights-based welfare system. His opposition was both theoretical and practical. His justification for welfare was derived from altruism: people should receive welfare as a gift from a 'stranger', as an expression of social solidarity rather than as an entitlement derived from a complex network of reciprocal obligations. This latter was far too redolent of individualistic society, with its self-interest and its anti-communal social arrangements. In a practical sense, he thought that the needy would lose out if welfare were to be completely translated into legal claims. Since each case is different, there has to be discretion in the delivery of welfare; indeed, officials deciding welfare problems should be seen as bearers of altruism rather than adjudicators between rivals in an adversarial context.

There are, however, good reasons why much of welfare philosophy focuses on rights, whether understood in universal or social terms. It is because their possession implies, in H.L.A. Hart's words, 'a special congruity in the use of force or threat of force to secure that what is just or fair or someone's right to have done shall in fact be done; for it is in just these circumstances that coercion of another human being is legitimate'.[15] If there are any welfare rights, then it can only be so if coercion can be justified in the redistribution of resources that their possession necessitates: welfare is not therefore justified in terms of benevolence but is a feature of entitlement or justice.

This demonstration would have two important consequences for welfare theory. First, welfare rights would be symmetrical with the familiar negative rights (i.e. rights to forbearance from aggressive action on the part of others). Secondly, it would, if successful, provide a plausible defence to the neo-conservative objection to the welfare state, that the very existence of welfare rights, enforceable at law, encourages people to adjust their behaviour accordingly, i.e. become welfare rights' claimants. The neo-conservatives then (in a decidedly un-liberal way) attribute 'blame' to such people. However, if welfare rights are symmetrical with negative rights, this sentiment may be inappropriate since people are entitled to whatever goods accompany them (in other words, there is no real problem of moral hazard here).

The liberal individualist objections to the assimilation of welfare (positive) rights to negative rights are well known and can be briefly summarized. A person's negative rights are honoured when others merely refrain from interference, whereas welfare rights require positive (deprivation-alleviating) action by others; since the satisfaction of positive rights necessitates a redistribution of resources, the rights of legitimate property-holders are thereby violated, hence welfare rights cannot properly be universal; the attribution of responsibility for the violation of negative rights is simple whereas it is impossible to assign the responsibility of meeting positive rights claims to anybody. A further argument is that because of the indeterminacy of positive rights they could be interpreted, at one extreme, as a claim for a massive worldwide redistribution of resources or, at the other, no more than the right to bare survival.

With the possible exception of the last point, it is now accepted, even by some neo-liberals, that the asymmetry between negative and positive rights cannot be demonstrated from the above considerations alone. The obvious point is that unless the right to life, for example, is interpreted simply as an injunction to refrain from killing with no implications as to how that right might be protected, the negative rights do involve positive action by the state in the provision of courts, police and so on; hence redistribution. Also, as Alan Hamlin[16] points out, a strict interpretation of the argument that it is morally permissible to protect only negative rights would entail a virtually unlimited expenditure on law and order and zero expenditure on welfare. The 'night-watchman' state, although limited, could still be very large.

However that may be, our concern now is to show that there are other reasons than those cited above which indicate that there is no exact symmetry between negative and positive rights. These hold apart from any practical reasons that tell against the assimilation of one to the other. The reasons cover the following issues: *indeterminacy, justiciability* and *responsibility*.

Indeterminacy is a problem because welfare rights theories say two potentially conflicting things: that a positive right to well-being is *more* than the entitlement to the minimum required for mere survival and that the needs on which it is based are objective. Thus even if it is agreed that well-being is essential to a developed morality, it is hard to see how its demands can be translated into the precise language of rights if it is to be a legitimate claim to more than a bare minimum. If one believes in the incommensurability and diversity of values, it is strictly impossible to incorporate the various 'well-beings' into one authoritative pattern. There is simply no agreement as to what 'needs' are for this notion to have that degree of objectivity which is required if it is to be the grounding of an uncontroversial right.

This problem of indeterminacy leads directly to the question of justiciability. It is understandable that welfare philosophers should demand the constitutional protection of welfare rights, since it is almost certainly the lax political rules of majoritarian democracies, and the discretion granted to officials, that have caused the failure of post-war welfare policies aimed at both equality and the relief of deprivation: coalitions of group interests have submerged the widespread desire for some form of welfare for the needy that exists in a community. Yet the demand for strict constitutional standards to prevent, for example, middle-class capture of the welfare state, is not the same thing as the demand for a 'list' of welfare rights (as in the UN Declaration of Human Rights). It is difficult to see how one could claim in a court of law that one's right to well-being had not been upheld by a government. It is true that many democratic states do include welfare claims and entitlements within their structures of positive law, but these derive from normal political processes and may very well be arbitrary. The claim is that it is difficult to see how a 'natural' or universal right to welfare could be incorporated into a basic constitutional document. It is worth pointing out that the most successful of the 'rights' documents, the European Convention on Human Rights (1950), says nothing about welfare.

The last difference between negative and positive rights centres on the question of personal responsibility for action. Does the fact that a person may act in such a way that they become *entitled* to welfare make a difference to their moral claim? This point has some practical application as contemporary welfare policies are known to encourage people to adjust their behaviour so as to secure an advantage. Alan Gewirth, who certainly believes in the symmetry of negative and positive rights, nevertheless stresses the fact that the agent 'cannot rationally demand of other persons that they help him to have basic well-being unless his own efforts to have it are unavailing'.[17] David Harris, a proponent of social rather than universal rights, similarly argues that: 'The fact of need, independently of how the need was created, does not provide a sufficient ground upon which a normative defence of need-meeting policies can be founded.'[18] Both these writers imply that questions of causal history and the direct attribution of responsibility for action are relevant to the moral status of positive rights. It seems to me that considerations such as these do point to a clear asymmetry between welfare rights and the familiar negative rights. For example, although we might say of a person that their action in walking through Central Park at 2.00 a.m. was extremely foolish, we would not say that this foolishness thereby rendered nugatory their right to forbearance from potential muggers.

The point is that we do not grant a welfare right automatically and the distinction between the two sorts of rights it alludes to has a practical application as well as a theoretical significance. For those critics of the welfare state who claim that it creates dependency rather than individual responsibility are challenging a basic tenet of welfare philosophy, i.e. that welfare institutions help to foster a less acquisitive agent than that which inhabits the apparently amoral world of competitive markets. It should be stressed that this objection holds quite independently of the cogency, or otherwise, of the other liberal argument, viz. that we cannot attribute deprivation-relieving responsibilities to the state under the guise of 'rights'.

Whatever is said about the cogency of welfare rights arguments, it does not follow that a rejection of them entails a rejection of the welfare state. For it is possible to argue that there is a duty, even of a compelling kind, for public institutions to relieve suffering. If the claim is put in this form, rather than in the form of indefeasible rights, some preconditions on the receipt of welfare, of the type specified by Gewirth and Harris, could be made.

There is, however, another, and more promising way in which a theory of welfare rights might be constructed; that is the contractarian method. There is every reason to suppose that rational contractors would choose a constitution that guaranteed a form of welfare, if only for insurance reasons. It is highly unlikely that such welfare provisions would be couched in the form of 'rights to wellbeing': they would emanate from an assembly charged with the function of delivering public goods. It is quite likely that a more 'efficient' form of welfare would be generated than that which emanates from conventional majority rule procedures. In this scenario there would obviously be no difference between negative and positive rights because everything would be a product of subjective choice, and would have value for that reason alone. But the rights that are granted would not be 'natural' rights.

IV

What is initially puzzling about the ethics of the welfare state is that a number of potentially conflicting values are used simultaneously to validate the typical welfare institutions and policies. The rights theory, despite its extension from negative rights (rights *against* government) to positive rights (rights to increased opportunities) is still fundamentally a liberal individualist theory, since it translates welfare statements into (ultimately) justiciable claims; yet, according to other welfare philosophers, it is this very language of rights that divides people from one another and disrupts those communal bonds that make welfare meaningful. Even apart from the embarrassing implication that a rights-based welfare philosophy could validate international transfers of wealth of a substantial kind, its implicit legalism seems to impede the growth of the altruistic, welfare sentiments.

It is for this reason that the ethics of the welfare state now grafts on to the notion of rights a theory of citizenship. This has the practical advantage of limiting the applicability of the welfare claim to particular communities and the theoretical one of establishing the identity of persons not by their capacity to choose but by their membership of collective entities, which are themselves the depositories of value. Communities, in other words, 'civilize' the market.

However, there is a subtle difference between a 'communitarian' and a 'citizenship' foundation of welfare. The former is an excessively vague concept. The supposition that there is a determinate set of values that 'binds' otherwise disparate individuals is not only highly contentious but, when filled out in specific details, is potentially oppressive of individuality. The phenomena that do the binding are as likely to be religious or racial than the concern to treat people equally as members of a common enterprise. Communitarianism seems opposed to that notion of liberal pluralism which maintains that people with different ends and purposes can be held together by submission to common rules.

Citizenship as a foundation for welfare is a little less ambitious: it simply maintains that claims to resources are an extension from the legal and political rights that have emerged in the development of liberal democracy. T.H. Marshall specifically placed the economic aspects of citizenship in an evolutionary account of the development of British society.[19] Three categories of citizenship are identified: legal citizenship, which embraces the traditional rights to free expression, property, equality before the law and the familiar civil liberties, most of which had been more or less established by the early part of the nineteenth century; political citizenship, covering the political rights in a democracy; and, finally, the citizenship of a welfare society that gives a person certain entitlements to resources. The rationale for citizenship lies in its capacity for the integration of all individuals into a society: for instance, the presence of economic rights that pertain to citizenship prevent class conflict (in the Marxian sense) getting out of hand. Although Marshall was by no means opposed to the market, he did see an unrestrained capitalism as socially destructive. Furthermore, it is probably the view of most citizenship theorists[20] that the categories are not self-contained but are only meaningful when taken as parts of a common social programme; thus the rights to free speech and legal equality require some measure of welfare if they are to be more than formal guarantees. Indeed, liberal pluralism is itself only possible when a measure of economic welfare is guaranteed.

Citizenship, with its relativistic appeal to prevailing standards and given ways of life as the source of rights, attempts to resolve the ambiguities in a purely abstract theory of welfare rights. If individuals are identified as abstract rational agents, and if it is this feature which entitles them to economic rights, then there really is no reason in principle why, if there are welfare rights, these should not be universalized across *all* rational agents. If, however, individuals are identified by their membership of a given social order

then that itself will contain ethical standards. In the absence of such
'objective' standards a society will be a mass of conflicting and irresolvable subjective values. In answer to the claim that need cannot
be a grounding for welfare, Harris writes that 'need is to be defined
in relation to the standards prevailing in society as a whole'.[21]

It might well be asked: what are they? It may be true to say that
a minority in a prosperous community who are the victims of more
or less permanent economic deprivation are not fully 'citizens', irrespective of their formal, legal qualifications, but this still leaves
open an enormously wide range of possible remedies for their condition. What is the connection between the needs defined by
citizenship and the collective delivery of, say, health, education,
pensions, and so on? The well-known inequalities that emerge
because of the welfare state (see Chapter 6) certainly privilege
some citizens over others. The problem is compounded by the fact
that most contemporary theorists of citizenship use this ethic to
found a liberal theory of rights, with all that the latter connotes in
the way of precision and justiciability. Yet compared to the entitlements implicit in the legal and political concepts of citizenship,
those in its welfare mutation are just not capable of an uncontroversial formulation. Furthermore, there are few theoretical limits
to the expansion of welfare rights under the rubric of this superficially anodyne normative social theory.

Despite the use of liberal language in citizenship theory there is
something illiberal at the heart of it. The attempt to establish the
ethical identity of persons by reference to 'ways of life' is potentially an *exclusive* doctrine. The criterion of identity, because it is
specifically not a universal feature of men but is a local and particular one, can be used as a barrier to outsiders, most obviously in
the enforcement of strict immigration rules. For if, legalistically, the
concept of citizenship includes welfare rights then this could easily
lead to a demand to limit the numbers of those entitled to claim
them. This is theoretically a problem for any welfare policy: a good
example is the US federal system where, on occasions, the variety
of welfare benefits available in different states led to migration to
the most generous, much to the resentment of the indigenous
inhabitants. It is especially troublesome for a citizenship theory
precisely because it includes costly and potentially divisive economic entitlements.

However, citizenship theory does highlight, in an oblique way, a welfare problem of modern society: the emergence of an 'under-class' of (possibly) permanently deprived people alongside growing prosperity for the majority. Whatever the welfare-enhancing properties of free exchange, it does seem to be accompanied by alienated groups ill-equipped for the kind of society it produces. This may have a 'feedback' effect on the more limited view of citizenship, which encompasses only legal and political rights, for the alienated groups may be, because of their economic deprivation, ill-suited to life in modern, abstract and anonymous societies.

An important question, though, is the cause of this phenomenon. Is it the case that welfare itself, as some critics maintain, is the cause of that dependency and lack of self-reliance that is apparent in some social groups in Britain and the USA, or do the 'cold' and impersonal relationships of the market simply fail to generate that loyalty which more intimate and simple societies display? The citizenship theory is an attempt to provide, through extensive welfare, a surrogate for this. Even if this were true, however, it does not at all follow that the existing welfare state policies and institutions are addressed to this. They are often a response to political pressure, brought about by electoral competition, rather than to the more elevated ethics of social solidarity. Citizenship theory is incomplete without an explanation of how the political system is to transmit a society's immanent moral values into satisfactory policies. Overall, there is the controversial question as to whether there is enough agreement over the economic implications of these values to validate their purported 'objective' status.

Justice, Equality and Welfare

I

It is disputed by some social philosophers that welfare should be the overriding goal of a society. Quite apart from the difficulty in locating a precise meaning to the concept, and the intractable problem of its measurement, there has always been a justified scepticism about the claim that all values form a kind of hierarchy with the welfare-maximizing injunction placed at the top. It has rightly been remarked that classical utilitarianism is implicitly totalitarian in its subordination of all other moral considerations to the welfare-maximizing imperative. Since all statements about collective welfare in this doctrine depend upon some kind of social computation in which the effects of alternative social policies on individuals are compared by (perhaps) an 'ideal observer', there has always been some tension between it and classical liberalism: a doctrine which in some versions, stresses the inviolability of individual rights.

The strong antistate welfare tradition in liberal thought largely derives from the claim that any statement that attributes good 'states of affairs' to a society, irrespective of individual desires, is fundamentally misconceived. The libertarian Robert Nozick put this point with his observation that:

> There is no social entity with a good that undergoes sacrifice for its own good. There are only individual people with their own individual lives. Using one of those for the benefit of others uses him and benefits the others.[1]

The prohibition on social welfare here derives from Nozick's invocation of negative rights as strong side-constraints on government action. From this it follows that justice must be limited to those procedural rules of a commutative and corrective kind that protect individual rights and justly acquired property.

However, this is not the only liberal position; indeed, its absence of any firm philosophical grounding for rights as side-constraints has limited its attractiveness. Furthermore, the rejection of all consequentialist considerations in moral evaluation means that not only it is vulnerable to the charge that it enjoins government inactivity in the face of 'catastrophes' but that it theoretically elevates one 'end', rights-protection, over all others, just as utilitarianism elevates a social maximand. A more plausible liberal argument is that in a complex society there is a variety of values and we have no a priori reason to rank any one over all others. One of these is, indeed, welfare so that individuals will require public institutions for its expression because of the familiar public-good problems that occur in the context of large numbers. Still, in this view it would not be the demands of redistributive justice that sanctioned welfare but those rules and procedures that translated people's subjective choice for it.

However, in contemporary political thought, justice has become almost inextricably bound up with welfare. John Rawls, in his *A Theory of Justice*,[2] insists that justice is the 'first virtue' of a society and that it should (almost) always take priority over the good (which may be interpreted in a welfare sense); there is certainly no pluralistic trade-off between the two. Yet Rawls's conception of justice is undoubtedly a welfarist concept, one specifically concerned with the legitimization of a distribution of resources and with levels of well-being. Indeed, despite its individualistic methodology, it is a normative theory that posits a welfare 'function' for society differing in substance, but not in principle, from other welfare functions, such as utilitarianism or the Pareto principle.

Still, Rawlsian justice is closer to liberal political economy than it is to collectivist welfare theory, especially in the latter's 'citizenship' and communitarian variants. This is so because he uses the contractarian method, a style of reasoning which purports to derive moral principles from the rational choices of abstract individuals deliberating under conditions of ignorance and uncertainty. He argues that a distribution of resources is just if it is to the benefit of the least advantaged. Inequalities are permissible to the extent that

they are necessary for the generation of a surplus for redistribution according to the Rawlsian formula. Individuals are not owners of their natural assets (talents), for these are the result of an arbitrary distribution of nature and therefore persons have no moral title to them. It is as if the bulk of the income derived from the exercise of talents constitutes unearned 'rent' so that this can be taxed away up to the point at which output is affected to the detriment of the least advantaged.[3]

It is in a very important sense an attempted solution to the property rights problem that lies at the heart of the liberal theory of welfare, i.e. the fact that 'efficiency' criteria are not relevant to the question of the initial distribution resources in a free economy. What makes Rawls a muted egalitarian is the fact that he extends the ethics of redistribution beyond the ownership of tangible property to the income derived from personal talents. Superficially at least, this seems to put the welfare imperative above the individualistic demand of justice.

Yet egalitarian though the implications of all this are, it is some way distinct from the ethics of the welfare state. For one thing, Rawlsian individuals are universal agents whose welfare claims derive from rational choice under conditions of ignorance and uncertainty; they are not members of particular communities with welfare entitlements that flow from a shared citizenship. Rawls's individualism is apparent here for it undercuts a claimed primary virtue of communitarian welfare theory, i.e. the existence of particularistic social bonds that give meaning to individual lives. Rawlsian individuals are abstractions, fleshless universal agents identified only by their capacity for rational choice and by their possession of a sense of justice. It is maintained that to locate individuals in known communities would be to give them information which would distort and bias their judgements. This has the awkward but logical implication that his redistributive criterion would require, in principle, massive transnational transfers to the least advantaged.[4] A redistribution to the deprived throughout the world would be regarded by a communitarian welfare theorist as a supererogatory duty rather than a strict obligation of justice.

A further significant point that differentiates Rawls is that his theory of justice is not concerned with the traditional welfare theory of objective need. There is no attempt to get behind his general redistributive rules to determine the typical needs that are visible in modern societies,[5] or to enquire into their causes. The 'least advantaged' is an abstract category, defined primarily in terms of income levels rather than some objective features of deprivation, such as permanent disablement or particular requirements (as education, healthcare or pensions). The principle that inequalities are permissible if they are to the benefit of the least advantaged is simply that 'safety-first' principle that rational individuals, who are ignorant of their circumstances, would adopt.

However, this manoeuvre may not necessarily be a vice, from a liberal point of view, since the incorporation of such infinitely extendable categories of need into a welfare scheme makes them subject to the vagaries of the political process, and there is no guarantee that redistribution to individuals in these categories will result from this. A Rawlsian redistribution rule, when described in less universalist terms, might well emerge from the subjective preferences that individuals have for welfare, as distinct from the preferences they express for *particular* welfare services, such as 'free' education, when they vote in competitive party democracy.

II

In the kind of reasoning proposed by Rawls, it might be possible to incorporate a welfare element into a theory of justice without violating liberal principles (although Rawls's claim that individuals are not the owners of their natural talents is quite at odds with that tradition). If the rules of society are the product of subjective choice, as they must be in Rawls's hypothetical contractarian method, then it is conceivable that rational contractors would choose a redistributive social policy. Uncertainty about the future might well motivate rational maximizers to opt for a set of rules that included some provision for the relief of their own possible future deprivation and its financing on insurance principles. Again, if the altruistic sentiment were a prominent feature of individuals' moral profiles, the contractarian method might reproduce it in some institutional and public form.[6] Whatever the reason for the emergence of a possible welfare rule, it would have the same obligatory force as normal legal and political rules precisely because it sprang from individual choice: the gap between welfare and justice would be closed.

However, there is a powerful (purist) liberal objection to the quasi-liberal project of the linking of justice and welfare. It derives

ultimately from the anticontractarian liberal tradition which holds
that the rules of justice develop spontaneously in response to
certain more or less universal features of the human condition, such
as scarcity, human vulnerability and limited altruism. It has been
developed in recent years by F.A. von Hayek. The argument
against the assimilation of justice and welfare here is not simply the
utilitarian one that a redistribution of income (on the grounds of
social justice) produces a misallocation of resources from which
everybody, including the worst off, suffers but a more complex one
about the meaning of justice and the nature of that moral responsibility which pertains to it.

Hayek objects to the very idea of social or distributive justice
because, in his view, justice and injustice can only be attributed to
the *intentional* actions of human agents under fair rules applicable
to everyone. Since society is not a 'person' it is absurd to speak of
it acting justly or unjustly.[7] The distribution of income that results
from the actions of individuals is not intended by any one person
so that no one can be morally responsible for it. In a famous
analogy, the results of market processes, because they cannot be
foreseen and are unintentional, are likened to the weather; no one
would, for example, claim that the distribution of sunshine between
the British Isles and Spain was 'unfair', precisely because it is an
unalterable fact of nature. Although Hayek, of course, does not
claim that distributions of income are quite like unalterable physical regularities, they are, he would say, 'natural' in the sense of not
being planned. And though they can be altered, such corrective
action will have unanticipated consequences.

Again, the familiar concept of 'desert' is irrelevant to the distribution of income, where desert or merit refers to the moral qualities of the recipient of income. In a market system, income received
is a function of the *value* of labour services (as measured by marginal productivity) and the recipient may display little in the way of
effort. In a complex society, there is simply no way in which a
planner could 'know' what the appropriate distribution of income
is and no hierarchy of moral values which could validate departures
from the non-moral values decreed by an anonymous market.

All interferences by political authorities with the anonymous
processes of exchange are not only inefficient in a utilitarian sense
but they are also arbitrary. They rest upon the mistaken assumption that there is a general agreement on deserts and needs in a

complex society when in fact there is none. Agreement about distributive ethics is only possible in an intimate, 'face-to-face' society where there is likely to be a common hierarchy of moral ends and a sense of solidarity that transcends the cash nexus and the scale of values determined by the market. In fact, Hayek regards the invocation of desert as an extra-market criterion of income distribution as a reversion to a primitive, tribalistic ethic quite at odds with the rationale of advanced societies;[8] they are purposeless collections of individuals held together by common rules rather than shared values.

It should be noted that this rather austere morality does not rule out a priori a version of welfare. Hayek concedes that some people will not be able to earn an adequate income because of the low or zero values of their labour and will have to receive extra-market payments: in fact, the higher productivity of an unimpeded market system should make this a comparatively minor problem. However, extra market payments of this type are not a matter of justice. The unfortunate, but not intended victims, of economic change do not have an entitlement to them because their distress is not a result of anyone's deliberate action. Welfare is presumably a matter of benevolence not justice, though this is not to deny that it can be compelling in some circumstances.

In a powerful critique of this position, Raymond Plant[9] has argued that, although the outcomes of a market process are, as Hayek describes, unintended, they can be foreseen. Furthermore, he claims that the meaning of justice is not simply a matter of how things come about, but how we *respond* to them. Thus, although no rule of procedural justice or fairness may have been breached in the course of market exchange, if the outcome of that process produces a distribution of income which leaves some in dire need then it would be an act of injustice, not merely a lack of benevolence, to do nothing. And, although society is not a person or a 'distributor', it has an agency, the state, which has the moral duty of alleviating alterable distress. The controversial assumption here is that *only* the state can fulfil such obligations.

It is certainly true that liberals capitalize on the proposition that the future course of economic events is unknowable, and that therefore interference with it is likely to produce unanticipated consequences. Also, the meticulous attention to the adverse consequences of the market's allocative process would require a degree

of knowledge of particular circumstances that could not be possessed by a central body. Nevertheless, the future, even to liberal
political economists, is not entirely unknowable and unforeseeable;
they are very confident of the effects of rent control, for example.
Although this is, of course, a government intervention, it is surely
not inconceivable that the effects of private economic change could
be foreseen, and their harms mitigated, in a similar way.

It is not clear what this argument implies for welfare philosophy
and policy. The periods of temporary unemployment that occur as
technology and tastes change can theoretically be catered for by the
insurance principle – which is, in theory, a liberal device, even
though it is compromised by the paternalistic element of compulsion in modern welfare states. If all foreseeable outcomes of market
processes were in principle insurable against, then it is difficult to
conceive of the market as a mechanism that causes deprivation and
which in turn generates a collective welfare responsibility.

There might, however, be a theoretical issue as to what level of
'compensation' is required by justice *in the absence* of satisfactory
insurance arrangements (can they ever be satisfactory?) It seems
plausible to suppose that the concept of strict justice, in the
context of foreseeable economic deprivation, has application only
to the uninsurable. But Plant writes that 'it is not clear that injustice is only a matter of how a particular outcome came about, but
rather is as much a matter of our response to the outcome'.[10] Presumably, then, because no one intended the patches of poverty in
the midst of plenty, there is a strict entitlement to welfare irrespective of insurance. Not to take action to alleviate economic
deprivation would be morally equivalent to failing to maintain law
and order.

However, it is also worth asking, in passing, the question as to
whether the irrelevance of the circumstances of origin of a welfare
problem would extend to the case of someone who, although quite
capable of insuring himself against misfortune, had wilfully failed
to do so. The question is actually hypothetical since a version of
compulsory insurance operates in Western democracies now.
Nevertheless, it raises an interesting problem for the theory of
justice, for if that now gives rise to a strict duty to relieve distress,
irrespective of how it came about, then justice is not solely descrip-
tive of reciprocal obligations between people but is really about a
general benevolence.

Even if we accept the applicability of the concept of justice to welfare there is the further question of whether it can be given any operational meaning in the ethics of income distribution. What level of extra-market payments are individuals entitled to as a matter of justice because of the vagaries and sometimes punitive effects of the exchange system? Is it to be subsistence or, as citizenship theory would imply, some relative share of the prosperity of a community? Presumably the latter, but it is hard to see what criteria could secure the kind of agreement that the demands of justice would require. The difficulty is that welfare philosophers want to found extra-market payments on something more compelling than benevolence; yet ideas of citizenship seem far too imprecise to satisfy that *strictness* which our ordinary notions of justice connote.

III

The social philosophy of welfare has been much concerned with *equality* itself: not the justification in rational terms of socially and economically necessary inequalities (which is a major concern of Rawls) or the identification and elimination of objective needs, but egalitarianism for its own sake. What R.H. Tawney called, in 1931, the 'religion of inequality', or the unthinking acceptance of that *mana* and *karakia*[11] of capitalist society, has been a constant source of criticism from welfare philosophers. However, welfare philosophy has not advocated an uncompromising egalitarianism, a Babeufist utopia in which all differences of wealth, income and status have disappeared, or a Marxist propertyless and classless order, but a system in which those legal and political equalities that the classical liberal has always valued are reflected in the economic world to a far greater extent than is possible under a capitalist market system.

Although the animus against the market that once powered interventionist welfare philosophy is less noticeable in contemporary thought, equality remains a potent value. Indeed it is argued that the virtues of *catallactic* (exchange) relationships are badly compromised if the participants in them are separated by gross disparities of wealth. One of those virtues is the market's capacity to expand freedom and choice: it is a neutral instrument that permits a wide variety of lifestyles to emerge and prosper and which, because of its fluidity, openness to innovation and change and its inherent unpredictability, prevents the dominance of some groups over others. However, since in capitalist societies some entrants to the market will start with advantages for which perhaps no rational justification can be given, this inequality will be reflected in the outcomes and results of the game itself. The joys of unpredictability will be soured and the market, instead of expanding the range of opportunities will merely replicate, by a kind of social genetics, the original inequalities.

Leaving aside for the moment the question as to whether this phenomenon is true, that markets under capitalist institutions cannot fulfil the ideals intrinsic to the exchange relationship, it is worth noting that if this approach is germane to contemporary welfare philosophy, it marks a significant change in ideology. For traditionally, that is from the New Liberalism of Green and Hobhouse to the altruism of Titmuss, the very idea of competition was treated with varying degrees of scepticism. A prevailing theme of welfare philosophy is that competitive relationships are necessarily uncooperative, their coldness and insensitivity to anything other than individual utility undermines fraternity, and they encourage divisiveness rather than unity. Too great a penetration of market principles into social life would undermine the welfare ethic itself. It is somewhat ironic that, in some welfare philosophies, the market should be not merely be praised for its efficiency, but also for its contribution, under special circumstances, to *equality* and freedom: Plant's work shows an explicit recognition of this.

The egalitarian aspects of markets had always been appreciated by liberal political economists. Perfectly competitive markets are in fact quite egalitarian: each factor of production is paid its marginal product, there is no 'wasteful' profit and the whole system is geared towards the satisfaction of the uncoerced wants of rational individuals. Even in the real world, as opposed to the texts of liberal economics, where there are (and in, some interpretations, must be) imperfections and excess profits, it is plausible to suppose that competition will be more effective than the state at eliminating them: Keynes's famous 'animal spirits' of capitalism may then be seen to be the unwitting promoters of a desirable end (just as Adam Smith had originally suggested). The upshot of all this is that those who believe in equality ought to recommend (*pace* Titmuss) a greater penetration of market principles into social life.

It has been known for some time that the state was an unreliable instrument for the promotion of equality. The welfare state in Britain has developed in a rather haphazard fashion with a variety of conflicting moral ends, and its activities have been justified by an equally variegated set of principles. More important, it has encouraged the growth of a complex set of vested interests, each with an incentive to exploit its provisions for named groups, rather than promoted an overall end of social welfare (however defined). So far from encouraging a spirit of altruism, the evidence is that the growth of collective provision of welfare services has provided new opportunities for the activities of the old *homo economicus*. Most important here is the phenomenon of behavioural adaptation: the ability of individuals to adjust their behaviour so as to become eligible for a welfare benefit. The aspects of human behaviour diagnosed by the creators of the Poor Law Amendment Act of 1834 have re-emerged in the twentieth century with renewed vigour (or perhaps have never been suppressed).

It is ironic that egalitarian thinkers, notably Julian Le Grand, should have been most assiduous in describing the seemingly ineluctable tendency towards inequality in the consumption of state-provided welfare services. Yet perhaps not surprising, since Le Grand has used the methods of the economist to explain this distressing phenomenon: the penetration of social welfare philosophy by economics nicely parallels the penetration of social life by the market so much criticized by the welfare philosophers.

In his *The Strategy of Equality*,[12] Le Grand subjected the claim of the egalitarian tradition (exemplified not just by Tawney but, more importantly, C.A.R. Crosland) that equality could be achieved not by the traditional socialist methods of public ownership and the breaking up of privilege at the foundational level (i.e. the distribution of property) but by the common consumption of welfare services – not subject to price and the demeaning means-testing associated with selectivity. Using a ratio of expenditure in the top fifth of the population, in income and occupational terms, to that of the bottom fifth, Le Grand found some alarming inequalities: in healthcare, the inequality was 1.4, secondary education for pupils over 16 years it was 1.8, non-university education 3.5, bus subsidies 3.7, university education 5.4, tax subsidies to owner-occupiers, 6.8 and rail subsidies, a spectacular 9.8.

As Le Grand has shown, the fact that a public service is available equally to all does not mean that it will be consumed equally: this will depend upon a whole range of factors that will vary across the population. As he says, there is almost a general principle at work: 'Policies involving subsidies whose distribution is dependent upon people's decision to consume the good or use the service favour the better off.'[13] Thus although healthcare is available equally to all at zero price, it is likely to be consumed more by middle-class individuals because the 'opportunity cost' (what they have to give up in order to consume) is much lower to them than to working-class patients; for example, they will not lose money from foregone work when they attend a doctor's surgery. The system of heavily subsidized higher education is notoriously productive of great inequality, and 'tax expenditures' on housing, as we have already noted, are the source of great inefficiency and inequity. Le Grand reaches the conclusion that, in some cases, it is likely that there would be greater equality if there was no public expenditure on the service concerned – an implicit recognition of the equalizing tendencies of the market.

No doubt classical liberals would argue that this could have been predicted on a priori grounds and that it implies some depressing but important conclusions. One such conclusion would be that certain behavioural traits are more or less universal so that to expect people to be 'moralized' by the presence of collective institutions and policies is simply utopian. Le Grand concurs with so much of the individualist's *methodology* that one wonders why he remains an egalitarian. His answer would be that the aim of equality can only be achieved by an attack on the fundamental sources of inequality in society – the distribution of resources and opportunities at the primary level.

Despite the obvious inefficiencies and inequities associated with state welfare services, they still have their defenders in the social welfare school. One argument is that, without middle-class participation, the poorest would be even worse off. Apparently, it is the constant middle-class political pressure ('sharp elbows') that keeps up public expenditure from which the poor benefit, almost by accident. This looks like a rather bizarre application of Adam Smith's 'Invisible Hand' thesis, i.e. that individuals, motivated by self-interest, unintentionally bring about a coordination of economic activities from which everybody benefits. It is the selfish consumption of education, health and so on, by the better off that ensures the survival of the welfare state for the benefit of the poor. Apart from the fact that this has a quite devastating implication for the argument that welfare institutions tap our resources of altruism, the theory is probably false. It is most unlikely that there would be no welfare state without middle-class participation *and* it is the case, empirically, that the middle classes use their 'sharp elbows' to protect services from which they benefit. Le Grand and Goodin claim that, in times of reduced government spending, it is those activities that have fewest middle-class users that are most adversely affected.[14]

The phenomenon of redistribution of welfare from rich and poor towards the middle-income groups is perhaps a special instance of a general rule of political behaviour in advanced Western democracies: the poor simply are not numerous enough to be decisive in electoral competitions. Ironically, the self-interest of both rich and poor groups dictates that they should form an alliance to prevent the adverse redistribution, but for many reasons, including ignorance, this has not happened and is unlikely to happen. What is puzzling is that, on the whole, *cash* redistributions (the technically most efficient type of egalitarianism) do continue under competitive party democracy, almost in defiance of the self-interest of the middle-income groups, and this must be because of a residual altruistic sentiment.

The general conclusion from all this is that constitutional and political considerations are of paramount importance in questions of redistribution. If there is an altruistic sentiment which would validate some of the activities of the welfare state, then existing political institutions are inefficient at transmitting it. There can be political failure as well as market failure. It is in recognition of this that some social philosophers have recommended the delivery of welfare in cash and strict constitutional protection for it from the vagaries of 'politics'. However, the potential and actual tension between the demands of welfare and existing democratic institutions has been insufficiently recognized in the social philosophy of welfare.

IV

There is still the question of why should the value of equality have the significance it has traditionally had in the philosophy of welfare? All societies seem to exhibit pretty regular inegalitarian features which seem more or less impervious to significant correction

by political methods, or else they are alterable only at a catastrophic cost in personal liberty. It may be the case that the egalitarian legal and political institutions of modern democracies are the
less effective to the extent that they are accompanied by economic
inequality. Perhaps wealth can 'buy' political power in defiance of
the merely formal equal rules of a liberal system. However, the
results of egalitarian social engineering have been shown to be dis-
appointing by egalitarian social scientists themselves.

The anti-egalitarian argument about welfare draws on distinction
between improving the *absolute* well-being of the worst off and
changing the *relative* positions of individuals in the income scale.
The moral imperative of the welfare philosophy should be directed
towards the former not the latter (even if egalitarianism were actually possible). This is indeed the implication of the nominally egalitarian social philosopher, John Rawls.

However, the more sophisticated egalitarian welfare theorist
argues that there is still a moral obligation to promote welfare
through egalitarian measures where this would not have such an
adverse effect on the output of an economy that the worst off would
suffer. Not to take action in such circumstances would be to acqui-
esce in a level of economic inequality which itself has adverse or
welfare-reducing effects on the rest of society. One possibility
would, of course, be a wealth tax, although the idea that there can
be a sufficiently high yield from this without being forced to extend
its range into portions of the community not considered to be extraordinarily wealthy is an illusion.

A more intriguing argument is that 'rental income' could be
taxed away without a loss of efficiency. Historically, the most familiar example is landownership. Since land is in more or less fixed
supply, and has little alternative use, part of the growing income of
an economy is absorbed by landowners with no productive activity
on their part. The same principle can be extended, although much
less plausibly, to occupations. If a person's income from their
present occupation is £1000 per week and the income from their
next best (which the person does not like much, we assume) is £400
per week, could not the difference be taxed away without affecting
work incentives? However, with a free international market in
labour, such taxation would presumably result in an exodus of
workers and hence efficiency (i.e. welfare) losses for the community.

There is a tradition in ethics, which Rawls's doctrine resembles in some ways, that does see the income from natural talents as a form of rent, i.e. 'undeserved', and hence suitable for costless redistribution. However, the theory is highly speculative and of dubious value in the construction of practicable welfare policies. Although the rental income from the ownership of land, about 12 per cent of gross national product (GNP) per annum, is a more plausible source of revenue, egalitarian philosophers have rarely investigated it.

7

Welfare, the Welfare State and Politics

I

The contemporary debate in Western societies has almost invariably been about the welfare state and the crisis in welfare philosophy is said to be a consequence of the difficulties typical welfare policies and institutions have experienced in the last twenty years. The slow-down in economic growth that occurred in the 1970s directed attention to the welfare state precisely because its founders had assumed that mixed economies would generate a level of national income sufficient to finance the services that had been justified on *ethical* grounds. Furthermore, although there were efficiency arguments that sanctioned some of the state-supplied welfare services, the primary aim of the welfare philosophers was redistributive: the common provision of education, health, unemployment insurance and so on, would itself be a mechanism both for the achievement of equality and the relief of deprivation. Overall there was the more elusive, and infinitely more contestable argument, that the institutions of the welfare state would generate forms of citizenship that soften and civilize those acquisitive and nontuistic attitudes that were held to be the defining characteristics of human action in market society.

Yet this assimilation of welfare theory to the philosophy of the welfare state was an intellectual error that had serious practical consequences. The theoretical mistake was the construction of a social philosophy that virtually ignored those welfare-enhancing properties of market systems that had been stressed by earlier liberal political economists. Furthermore, those earlier writers on welfare, primarily utilitarians and *laissez-faire* theorists of the nineteenth century, were sceptical about the ability of government to promote welfare without at the same time generating unintended and unwelcome side-effects, for example, the encouragement to dependency that extensive state welfare would produce. This latter argument depended on there being more or less universally true features of the human condition which were either suspended or ignored by theorists of state welfare.

The serious practical consequences that resulted from the assimilation of welfare to state welfare were the seemingly inexorable expansion of the welfare state and the well-documented evidence that, in all Western democracies, it had mutated from a system designed to protect the vulnerable from the sometimes random effects of market forces to a comprehensive set of social arrangements which had only a contingent connection with the original purpose of interventionism. This arose largely because of the failure of theorists of the welfare state to take proper account of the institutions that are required for the delivery of the welfare good: there can be no guarantees, for example, that the outcomes of a competitive party process in a democracy will coincide with the moral imperatives of state welfare theory. There is a serious problem as to whether majority-rule procedures are *efficient* in the translation into positive policies of whatever altruistic sentiments exist in a community.

II

The assimilation of the concept of welfare to the typical institutions and policies of the welfare state, however, has also occasioned an intellectual debate which is remarkable for its *theoretical* components. Thus it is no longer exclusively a social science or empirical enquiry into the selection and evaluation of those facts which are relevant to the solution of problems that occur within an agreed welfare paradigm, but one which involves fundamental challenges to the paradigm itself. Although a minority of social theorists has always existed that challenged the basis of the welfare state and preferred to restrict the use of the concept to the description of individual experiences of well-being that are realized in market exchanges, or any other form of voluntary action that takes place independently of the state, throughout much of this century there was something of a consensus about the necessity for some state welfare – a consensus whose rationale lay precisely in the claim that there were genuine collective welfare ends which could not be met through voluntary action. This consensus embraced theorists of remarkably different theoretical perspectives, ranging from liberal individualists, who claimed that state welfare was a type of public good (the provision of which satisfied subjective individual desires), through to socialists of one sort or another who claimed that collective provision was a necessary feature of social justice.

What is important about the contemporary attack on the welfare state is that, although its most vociferous and articulate exponents have come from the 'Right' of the intellectual and political spectrum, it has been directed as much against conventional neo-liberal and conservative nostrums (one example, to be considered below, is the 'Negative Income Tax') as it has been against the more conventional socialist ideology of state welfare. A further complication is the fact that such is the protean nature of the concepts of welfare and the welfare state that it is difficult to disentangle just what is being specifically criticized in the current debate. Is it the very ideas of welfare itself, the theory that, in principle, some redistribution of resources through the state is sanctioned by moral theory which is objectionable? Or the complex plethora of institutions and policies that constitute the welfare state that is condemnable for its inefficiency and inequality?

Again, the problem is compounded by the fact that the principles which underlay the critique of the welfare state are various, still somewhat inchoate, and always contestable. This last feature is most conspicuous in the argument that the existence of a welfare state, because it involves coercion, necessarily reduces freedom. However, this objective depends on it being true that freedom means absence of restraint. Yet a whole tradition of welfare thought claims that social and economic deprivation, by *causing* individuals to act in certain ways, is itself liberty-reducing. Thus an argument about welfare is quickly transformed into an argument about freedom, and the same process seems to be at work when other principles, for example, rights, equality and justice, are invoked. Nevertheless, inconclusive in any ultimate theoretical sense though the contemporary criticisms of the welfare state may be, they have at least pointed to some important theoretical issues and explicated key problems in the concept of welfare – problems that are not confined to the liberal individualist's critique of the welfare state itself.

Almost all of the discussions about state welfare are ultimately of a utilitarian kind. The concept itself is precisely about well-being and the various instrumental means by which 'satisfaction' of one kind or another may be brought about. It is true that there have been arguments that ethics and political philosophy are not about well-being at all but about the restraints that should govern political action, and from the existence of such restraints welfare-enhancing action by the state is excluded. The most notable contemporary example of this is Robert Nozick's *Anarchy, State and Utopia*, in which the 'nightwatchman state' is precluded from any welfare activity.

Although the terms in which Nozick writes, i.e. the invocation of absolute and inviolable individual rights, puts him outside the contemporary welfare debate, his rigorous individualism and anti-statism alerted social theorists to the possibility that many welfare goals could be satisfied outside the formal apparatus of government. His political theory is not founded upon the rather *passé* distinction between the market and the state but between freedom and coercion. This leaves open the theoretical possibility that voluntary activity outside the price mechanism could solve at least some of today's welfare problems. Hence, perhaps the most important part of *Anarchy, State and Utopia* may turn out to be the last section, 'A Framework for Utopia',[1] in which the chief virtue of the limited state is said to lie in the permission it grants to individuals to pursue differing ways of life. Given the dissatisfaction that collectivists have expressed for the conventional structure of the welfare state, it is important to stress the fact that *other* institutional arrangements are possible for the public expression of that non-selfish sentiment upon which all welfare policy depends.

III

The critique of the assimilation of welfare to state welfare nevertheless emerged from rather more prosaic considerations than the abstract moralism of natural rights theories. The experience of the post-war welfare state in Western democracies has cast doubt on, not just the ethical desirability of entrusting collective institutions with the delivery of what have come to be called the typical welfare services, health, insurance, education, housing and so on, but also the efficacy of this method. The seemingly inexorable expansion of these services, and an increasing share of gross domestic product (GDP) absorbed by them, has led to serious criticism from both Left and Right of the political spectrum, suggesting that the foundations of the system are shaky. What is significant from the point of view of political theory is that the arguments about state welfare are by no means novel but are embedded in both the history of welfare state institutions and the principles that have historically validated them.

The difficulty arises primarily over a confusion at the very heart of the theory of the welfare state itself – a confusion between the conception of the state's role as a provider of a minimum standard of well-being for those individuals who cannot cope adequately in market society and a broader conception that envisages collective institutions as prima facie appropriate for the satisfaction of a potentially limitless range of human wants. The problem of welfare is then simply a variant of the most familiar problem in political theory, the legitimate contents of the agenda of the state. The extension of the welfare state from a minimalist to maximalist state has drawn attention to this in a particularly stark way.

In what sense can the common provision of, say, education and health, enhance welfare in the sense understood by the philosophers of the welfare state? The welfare state is characterized by what public economists call 'churning',[2] whereby the services are funded by tax revenue which are then 'returned' to the citizens in the form of collective and often compulsory services (e.g. unemployment insurance). It is not quite clear what the rationale for this is. From the strict Paretian standpoint, the claims for its efficiency hardly look compelling since the compulsory nature of many features of the welfare state means that individual choice is suppressed; thus the actual structure of the system does not reflect people's preferences. Only if some feature of the exchange system prevented these choices being recorded could it be said that, theoretically, the state could make the familiar efficiency improvements.

This might be so in the case of healthcare where the private insurance system may be responsible for some undesirable phenomena.[3] The most common complaint is that it may cause the *oversupply* of health. A person who has paid their premium has an incentive to demand 'excess' treatment since the marginal cost to them is zero;

and, of course, the doctor is equally encouraged to supply it. The ensuing escalation of health costs then leads to a situation in which patients are worse off through the higher premiums that result. If we add to this the resource costs (which occur through excessive litigation) that insurance-based medicine undoubtedly encourages, then a strong case could be made for state intervention here on efficiency grounds. The argument becomes even stronger when the problem of the 'uninsurable', victims of the arbitrary forces of nature, is considered. Any efficiency criteria that failed to take account of this phenomenon would have a poor claim to welfare irrespective of the purity of its derivation from individual choice.

Yet even this – one of the most plausible of the cases for the necessity of the assimilation of welfare to state welfare – is by no means uncontroversial. The incorporation of healthcare into a *compulsory* system simply converts the problems associated with private choice into those of public choice.[4] It seems to be the case that individuals as *voters* regularly choose a lesser amount of expenditure on healthcare than they would be prepared to pay for as consumers. This is largely because of phenomenon that, to each voter, lower taxation in the short run is more attractive than expensive healthcare in the long run. The problem here is that, while on the one hand a welfare philosophy that granted a 'right' to healthcare would, morally at least, sanction an almost unlimited claim on a community's resources for this purpose, the vote-maximizing process tends, perhaps equally inexorably, to lead to an undersupply. Indeed, from a purely subjectivist position, is it possible to 'know' what an optimal supply of healthcare is?

Again, if the rationale of the assimilation of welfare to the welfare state is sanctioned by the demands of social justice, the democratic system itself is an unreliable mechanism for the achievement of this, even if social justice were a legitimate political goal (itself a highly contestable proposition). We have already seen that empirical enquiries into the delivery of welfare services in Britain produces a redistribution towards middle-income groups, and there is reliable evidence that it is a universal feature of democratic societies.[5] In fact, this phenomenon is predictable from a more general 'theorem' of political economy known as 'Director's Law'.[6] Put at its simplest, this law holds that, since in an advanced Western democracy the probable majority of voters is neither (comparatively) rich nor poor, whatever redistribution that takes place is likely to go to it. Bizarre though it sounds, the only possible way that this could be countered would be an electoral alliance between rich and poor – a most unlikely occurrence as we have noted (see Chapter 6).

Perhaps the most decisive objection to the assimilation of welfare to the welfare state turns upon the question of the causal explanation of the existence of welfare problems. The rationale of the welfare state has, ever since its inchoate structure was embodied in the Poor Law, rested upon the assumption that voluntary arrangements, either by the market system of insurance or by charity, would be inadequate. Although early critics of state welfare pointed to the possibility that the existence of state welfare itself could create the problems that it was designed to solve, this did not become a serious intellectual issue until after comprehensive welfare states had been established in Western democracies in the mid-twentieth century.

However, in recent years, the debate has concerned this very issue. The claim that state welfare may have counterproductive effects takes many different forms and it is not always clear what is meant by it. One familiar suggestion, derived from pessimistic individualistic assumptions of human nature, is that the supply of welfare at zero, or near zero, price simply draws forth an increased demand, just like a normal economic good; another is that well-intentioned welfare policies help one group while unintentionally harming another (familiar examples are rent control which, by freezing the supply of rented accommodation, causes homelessness; and minimum wage legislation, which renders unemployed potential workers whose marginal productivity is lower than the decreed minimum). A more ethical argument is that excessive welfare produces a dependency culture which is quite inconducive to good citizenship. What is of crucial importance is the fact that these structures are directed as much to the purely liberal theory of welfare, which justifies the relief of deprivation on quasi-technical public-good grounds, as it is to the specifically non-economic theories of state welfare based on an expanded citizenship and the varieties of social justice.

IV

The hitherto scarcely articulated theoretical issues that permeate the whole of the welfare state system were brought to the fore in the thorough analysis and intense debate that followed the creation of the 'Great Society' in the USA by President Johnson's administration. This was a massive programme of welfare intervention that came to fruition in the 1970s. It has provided a good test case for many critics of state welfare. It cost about US$200 billion per year, and through a variety of institutional arrangements at federal and state level it delivered 44 major programmes, including Medicaid, AFDC (Aid to Families with Dependent Children) and food stamps, to about 50 million people. It should be stressed that the designers of these schemes had no real desire to create a 'welfare society' in which individuals were permanently tied to collective arrangements through communitarian bonds (which is a common justification for public welfare provision), but rather envisaged the measures as temporary but necessary aids to the achievement of individual autonomy in the traditional American sense. It was meant to be a 'hand-up' rather than a 'hand-out' and recognised a distinction between welfare and the welfare state.

Implicit in the rationale for all this was the argument that capitalism was the cause of deprivation – a plausible assumption, given that one-third of Americans were said to be below the official poverty line in 1950, i.e. before the implementation of *comprehensive* welfare programmes in the USA. Also, certain identifiable groups, especially the ethnic minorities, were thought to be especially victimized by this causal process. Hence the whole battery of legal and institutional arrangements to improve their position within the context of traditional American institutions and values.

There is some agreement between observers that the system has not fulfilled its aims. Although the numbers in poverty have been reduced, this is not because more people have achieved individual autonomy but because more have become dependent on the new welfare payments. Charles Murray, in an influential study,[7] makes a distinction between people in poverty, a straightforward measure of those who fall below a specified standard of well-being, and those in 'latent poverty', individuals who would be deprived were it not for the existence of state welfare. He reports that between 1950 and 1965, latent poverty fell from about one third of the population to about 18 per cent. However, as the Great Society programmes began to take effect, the figures began to rise: latent poverty rose to 19 per cent in 1972, 21 per cent in 1976 and had reached 22 per cent by 1980. Similarly distressing figures were reported for employment of deprived minorities, especially blacks, who were also the accidental victims of minimum wage laws. Murray also specifically linked the breakdown of traditional family structures and the rise of illegitimacy to the new benefits for unmarried mothers. There seems then to be evidence of 'moral hazard' on a massive scale.

Although there is some dispute about the figures, most commentators argue at least that the Great Society programme has failed to reduce the number on welfare; indeed, similar phenomena are observable in other Western democracies, including Britain. Irrespective of the statistical argument, the whole issue involves fundamental questions of welfare philosophy, for it raised in an uncanny way precisely those principles that were predominant in the welfare debate of the 1830s and in the early part of the twentieth century: social causation, dependency, rights, justice, individual and social responsibility, and so on.

In some philosophies, empirical evidence about the counter productive effects of welfare are not (logically) relevant. If the argument is that individuals have a right to welfare – in the strict sense of an enforceable claim against the community, equivalent to a right to forbearance in that it requires no particular action on the part of the holder of the welfare right – then individuals who are 'attracted' to welfare are simply claiming that to which they are entitled. However, it is doubtful if welfare theorists would want to extend this 'right' to the whole panoply of services that happen to be provided collectively. Almost all would want to place conditions, at least beyond a certain level of provision, on the receipt of welfare, conditions that would be designed to prevent the possibly infinite expansion of a form of welfare that demanded no social obligations on the part of the recipient.

In fact, Murray's strictures are addressed most pertinently to the classical liberal's theory of state welfare. Although all classical liberal theorists are aware of the counterproductive effects of state welfare (indeed they formulated most of the objections), the logic of their theory leaves them just as vulnerable as the rights theorists. The liberal individualists, Hayek and Friedman, for example, believe in pluralism and the ultimate subjectivity of human values: there is no 'right way' of living or hierarchy of principles which ought to be imposed upon people. Indeed, that is just one of their objections to a redistribution derived from the so-called objective values of desert and need. Hence, the occurrence of a dependency culture and a welfare ethic cannot be, strictly speaking, the source of their objections to the extended welfare state. After all, the rationale for some welfare lies just as much in the fact that it raises the utility of the donors (normally taxpayers) as it does the recipients. The Negative Income Tax is favoured by classical liberals precisely because it is an income supplement not tied to any 'desirable' form of expenditure: to link it to such things as pensions, health, housing, and so on, would be to impose a particular conception of the good on individuals.

Yet, as Murray reports, where experiments with the Negative Income Tax were tried in the USA, they produced the worst results of all in terms of defection from work, marital breakdown, and so on. But this is only an extreme case of a system of welfare that imposes little or no social obligations on the citizens. In fact early critics[8] of the Negative Income Tax had argued that it would in effect produce a new 'Speenhamland system' because its potentially open-ended commitment to cash payments divorced from any moralistic notions of 'deservingness' would prove too great a temptation to individuals. Indeed, the utilitarians who devised the Poor Law Amendment Act of 1834, with its harsh 'less eligibility' requirement or 'workhouse test' showed themselves to be more realistic than their libertarian successors in the twentieth century, however unpalatable to the modern mind their solutions to the welfare problem were.

Murray's discussions of the increase in welfare 'take-up' that occurred in the USA in the 1970s echo precisely this earlier debate. His main argument is that it is not the actual value of welfare benefits that is crucial (in fact they declined in real terms throughout the 1970s), but the ease with which a person could become eligible for them. Although part of the reduction in eligibility requirements relates specifically to the American experience (such as Supreme Court decisions that struck down state residency rules for welfare and allowed payment to unmarried mothers who were living with men), the bulk of the argument is addressed to a general feature of all welfare schemes, the inducement to high take-up when they are in the form of cash. Murray's further argument, that the Great Society reforms were based on a faulty analysis of human nature, bore a striking resemblance to propositions espoused openly in the 1830s. He maintained that contemporary social theorists of welfare overlooked or ignored three basic propositions of human nature: people respond to incentives and disincentives; they are not naturally industrious or moral; and that if society is to function, individuals must be held responsible for their actions.[9]

Thus although Murray may have established one element in the classical liberal's theory of welfare, i.e. that the state is a more decisive causal agent in the emergency of welfare problems than the market, he also undermined the particular liberal solution to whatever problems there might be – the payment of cash unencumbered by moral considerations. Of course, it is always open to the proponent of the Negative Income Tax to insist that the cash payment is simply too high and that the attractiveness of work would be greater if the income supplement were drastically lowered. But how low would it have to fall to produce the desired effect? Again, would the voting system disrupt the 'rational plans' of individualistic social philosophers?

The point made by Murray, and other critics of the assimilation of welfare to state welfare, is that the problem is not really about money, or perhaps only partially so, but more to do with more traditional notions of self-esteem and personal autonomy. Thus, although the market system may reduce a person's freedom in the sense of autonomy by reducing the range of options, for example, in times of high unemployment, the state system can do so much more effectively. His solution, though he concedes that it is not politically practicable, would be to reduce drastically the level of state welfare, for it is this he claims, that generates 'cycles of deprivation' and a more or less permanent underclass. Yet he remains more or less in the classical liberal tradition in that his solution to the welfare problem is *small government*, rather than the inculcation of desirable values; these will emerge, presumably, spontaneously in the absence of welfare.

This is subtly different from what might be called the conservative response to the welfare problem, for this does not reject the case for state involvement on individualistic grounds at all but, in effect, rejects the 'value-neutrality' of liberalism itself. It is in this argument that there is a meeting of minds between conservative and socialist theories of citizenship. Both would maintain that the ideal of citizenship does grant individuals a claim on the resources of a community but that it must be accompanied by corresponding social duties. Thus individuals are not anonymous agents held together by general rules of just conduct and the cash nexus but are identifiable members of particular communities, defined in terms of a complex network of social rights and duties.

Thus Lawrence Mead's[10] objection to the American welfare system is not to its size but to the fact that its benefits are distributed as *entitlements* requiring no duties on the part of the beneficiaries. In fact, he specifically isolates the American 'Lockean' tradition of liberalism, with its indifference to civic virtue, as the cause of the malaise. The Lockean remedy of small government and the drastic curtailment of welfare is quite inadequate since the penetration of American society by the 'welfare as entitlement' ethic has rendered significant numbers of the population incapable of responding in the predicted individualistic way. What is required then is, ironically, a stronger, and perhaps bigger, state to enforce the social obligation of *work* that is correlative of the receipt of welfare, and *less* freedom. Mead puts the point graphically with his claim that 'work must be treated as a social obligation, akin to paying taxes and obeying the law'.[11] Workfare irrespective of its cost, becomes the twentieth century surrogate for nineteenth-century eligibility tests.

To the classical liberal, or indeed those egalitarian liberals, such as Rawls, who wish to equalize access to opportunities without at the same time abandoning the pluralistic ideal idea that the state should be neutral towards differing ways of life, these words may sound a little chilling. However, the principles of conduct that they express are necessary inferences from a coherent theory of citizenship. These considerations also show that the theory of welfare that derives from citizenship has its intellectual origins in that mutation out of classical liberalism, 'social liberalism', first articulated philosophically by T.H. Green and L.T. Hobhouse, writers who would certainly not have regarded welfare rights as entitlements involving no correlative social obligations. Thus although those writers, especially Green, tried to redefine liberty so that it was not inconsistent with both redistribution through the state and binding social obligations, this was an unnecessary and confusing linguistic manoeuvre. The existence of an extensive range of welfare institutions and policies is not compatible with negative liberty and pluralism.

To reinforce this incompatibility of welfare and liberty thesis, it is even possible to trick out a justification for an equally illiberal (in the conventional sense) supply of welfare from at least one variety of the typical Paretian justification of the welfare state. It will be recalled that the rationale for Paretian redistribution to the deprived rested on the not unreasonable assumption that donors received satisfaction from the relief of suffering, i.e. the utility gains were not to the beneficiaries only. It was the presence of the familiar public-good problem that prevented an optimum being reached by voluntary (charitable) methods. However, it is surely plausible to suppose, on purely subjectivist grounds, that the donors' utility is partly a function of the form in which welfare is delivered.[12] They might very well regard themselves as adversely affected by the existence of cash payments enshrined in the Negative Income Tax, untied to any specific form of expenditure. They might then demand that welfare expenditure be in the form of housing, education, pensions, and so on. Equally, they might be aggrieved that their transfers were being consumed by individuals under no specific social obligations of the type demanded by, for example, Mead's version of citizenship.

The fact that the most articulate exponent of the Negative Income Tax, Milton Friedman, argues that it should not be tied to any particular form of 'desirable' expenditure or accompanied by social obligations, is a tribute to his own rationalistic, individualistic and determinedly antipaternalist liberalism. It is not really a contribution to the welfare problem identified by contemporary writers, some of whom would not be unsympathetic to the more general political position he espouses. It is now contended that the problem with the poor is not the simple one that 'they do not have enough money', but a more complex one involving intricate questions of self-fulfilment, citizenship and what it is to lead a worthwhile life. It is recognised that the problem of the emergence of an 'underclass' – a minority of individuals deprived of a share in growing prosperity and alienated from the rules and morality of the society that generates it – involves complex questions of causation. It is soluble neither by an ever-widening range of state-supplied services nor by the naive and superficially 'liberal' nostrum of cash redistribution.

V

It is apparent to many observers that welfare in the sense of individual personal well-being (or, indeed in the more controversial sense of social welfare) is not necessarily enhanced by overreliance on the state. This is not a political judgement but a theoretical one about the meaning of statements about welfare, and about the conditions that may plausibly be said to obtain if it is to be advanced. For a person's welfare is advanced in ways other than mere increases in income; it is as much a function, for example, of personal esteem and individual autonomy. Critics of the welfare state have such non-economic measures of value in mind when they comment on interventionist measures, of whatever type, which have a tendency to produce dependency and an antiwork ethic. It is the necessarily *subjective* nature of welfare that makes the question of what constitutes an improvement in well-being so intractable.

Furthermore, given the competing demands of the typical welfare goals, relief of indigence, education, housing, pensions, and so on, and given the absence of any objective principle, or hierarchy of principles, by which these demands can be ordered, the assimilation of welfare to the welfare state must result in the imposition of one set of priorities over others. Whether this emanates from the will of a benevolent 'dictator' (which is the implication of nineteenth-century utilitarianism, as revealed in the welfare philosophy of Edwin Chadwick) or from the possibly arbitrary processes of democratic politics, is immaterial to this subjectivist problem. Thus, whereas at one time there was an agreement, which transcended party affiliations, that the relief of indigence was the primary goal of welfare policy, the expansion of the state into other areas, which have little to do with this, has proceeded with a much more contestable claim to public authorization.

A major part of the problem of the welfare state is not simply the lack of agreement as to what its priorities should be, but a further confusion of two separate justificatory principles. These are the insurance principle and the welfare principle itself. The former is in fact a market principle and is, of course, not germane to the original rationale of welfare policy, the relief of avoidable suffering. However, in important areas, the insurance function of economic society has been largely taken over by the state. And in doing this, many critics have claimed that it has neglected its welfare role, i.e. the relief of indigence.

It is not difficult to see why the insurance principle should have been so attractive to the twentieth-century architects of the welfare ideal. The main reason is that it incorporates the idea of entitlement to the receipt of benefits, removes any trace of stigma attached to welfare and *in theory* provides an economic check on a potentially limitless expansionary process of state expenditure. For these reasons, the provision of state insurance schemes is not markedly inconsistent with liberal philosophy. Of course, typical state insurance schemes, unemployment, health and pensions, for example, are compulsory but even that strikingly illiberal policy has always had a plausible justification, i.e. those individuals with high time preferences will not insure themselves against the vicissitudes of life so that they present a welfare problem anyway.

This issue is surely an extremely good example of the market versus the state 'contest', for it cannot be assumed a priori that private insurance is the universal solvent of all welfare problems, as the example of medicine in the USA, cited earlier in this chapter, shows. However, the same political problems that beset the more familiar welfare state institutions are, historically, not absent from the 'insured' elements of welfare provision. In almost all cases the insurance element becomes quickly a fiction and the services become, to all intents and purposes, tax financed. Thus, instead of the recipients of such benefits receiving that to which they are entitled, in an economic or actuarial sense, they become the beneficiaries of *redistributive* taxation. However, it is an inefficient form of redistribution, in a welfare sense, since it is not addressed necessarily to those in deprivation but to those who happen to be in the nationalized insurance system. It is for this reason and others that the welfare state in its comprehensive form is unlikely to 'wither away' with growing prosperity, a dream in fact shared by many of its founders, since individuals of necessity become 'dependent' on it in a way that does not reflect those moral concerns identified by Mead and Murray. They become entitled to benefits even though their contributions do not, in a strict economic sense, sanction this.

The most spectacular example of this phenomenon in Western democracies is the provision of old age pensions by the state. It was Alfred Marshall, by no means a fanatical advocate of *laissez-faire*, who first noted the dependency-enhancing effect that state pensions had. He wrote, in 1905, that 'universal pensions . . . do not contain . . . the seeds of their own disappearance. I am afraid that, if they started, they would tend to become perpetual'.[13] However, as the twentieth century developed, the situation worsened with the emergence of earnings-related and unfunded pension schemes which are now posing serious economic, political and ethical problems for contemporary liberal democracies, especially the USA and West Germany, but also Britain, though to a lesser extent.[14] Their existence constitutes the best example of two interrelated incoherencies in welfare theory: the confusion between insurance and welfare and that between limited intervention to aid the poor (and uninsurable) and comprehensive arrangements involving compulsory welfare for all. Again, it is the assimilation of welfare to state welfare that has spawned unintended malign consequences, even though they could have been, and indeed were, anticipated.

Although superficially it looks as if state provision for the elderly is a perfect case of legitimate welfare activity by the state (historically there was a close correlation between being old and being poor) closer analysis reveals that this is not necessarily so. In principle, there is in fact nothing special about pensions, i.e. nothing about them which necessitates state involvement on either (economic) efficiency grounds or ethical grounds (as part of a general moral obligation to relieve avoidable indigence). Pensions are simply deferred wages and are paid from savings accumulated during the working life. Their value in theory represents people's time preferences, i.e. how much of present consumption they are prepared to sacrifice for consumption in the future. There is no reason in theory why a competitive insurance market should not offer a variety of arrangements to cater for people's differing time preferences. To *force* people to save a specific amount for the future is, *prima facie*, to undermine people's freedom and autonomy in the sense defined by the moral philosophers of welfare – it is to determine, arbitrarily, the pattern of consumption over their lives.

The only plausible rationale for state compulsion would derive from moral hazard, i.e. if the state does have a moral obligation to relieve suffering, then people may be induced to raise their consumption and reduce saving now on the understanding that there will be adequate provision for their retirement. Hence, to avoid this phenomenon, the state should compel them to save while working. However, this argument depends upon the highly dubious assumption that individuals do have higher time preferences than the officials of the state driven by the vote motive. It is difficult to derive a case for compulsion and uniformity from the demands of social justice since, whatever might have been the case historically, being old now is not the same thing as being poor. Indeed, in an imaginary society in which individuals began with equal resources, one would predict that there would be inequality between the old and the young as assets are accumulated over a working lifetime. Apart from a minority who are not favoured by earnings-related pensions, the old are comparatively wealthy.

Yet despite these considerations, state involvement in pensions has created massive problems for the future and very little of its activity here has been directed towards the genuine welfare problems of the uninsurable and others unable to cope with life in market society. What has been called the impending 'pensions catastrophe' has been caused by the practice of guaranteeing earnings-related old-age pensions, not through properly-funded schemes in which payment to retirees represents genuine lifetime saving, but through 'pay-as-you-go' arrangements. Those latter are direct tax transfers from the present working generation to retirees, a process (allegedly) morally validated by the existence of a quasi-contract between the generations by which the process is continued indefinitely into the future. Furthermore, when these transfers are earnings-related, they preserve into retirement the inequalities of the prevailing income structure.

This system would not be catastrophic in a kind of 'equilibrium' world where economic growth rates, demographic facts and the ratio of young to old, are perfectly stable and predictable. Pensions, including an earnings-related element, would be paid as part of a general welfare scheme. There might be objections to this on grounds of its freedom- and autonomy-reducing features, but the economic knowledge on which it is based precludes that *intergenerational inequity* which real-world unfunded schemes generate. This phenomenon is likely to occur because of uncertainty about future growth rates and demographic conditions. If population growth slows down and if people live longer, as they are likely to do given improvements in medicine, then, under 'pay-as-you-go' arrangements, a declining workforce is legally (and morally?) obliged to support expanding numbers of retired people. Normal public choice assumptions strongly imply that individuals have every incentive to keep the system going through fear of 'writing-off' their own tax 'investments' in the system if they were to renege on the implicit contract. It is a strange morality which permits the imposition of burdens on one generation, without its consent, in order to satisfy the wants of an older one, irrespective of the normal welfare criterion of need. It is, indeed, an ironic twist to Rousseau's famous dictum that 'man is born free but is everywhere in chains'. Now, people are born burdened with debt.

It is argued[15] that funded schemes suffer from the same disability as 'pay-as-you-go' arrangements since, although they pay out nominally an income which has been earned through past saving, they too depend on the productivity of future generations and are therefore equally vulnerable to the demographic and other factors that determine this. However, funded schemes involve investment in the economy which leads to a deepening and lengthening of the capital structure, i.e. the growth of 'roundabout' methods of production which yield in the long run more consumer goods. Most American economists agree that had contributions to the US social security system been invested on the stock market there would have been significantly higher productivity in the economy and therefore retirement pensions of higher value.[16] At present, it is reckoned that there is an unfunded legal liability of US$8 trillion in the USA, a debt that can only lead to very high social security taxes in the next century. As the authors of a recent study of the problem of 'age' in the welfare state point out:

> medium and higher income young adults learn that the welfare state has little interest in them, except as funders of the benefits of earlier generations.[17]

The theoretical implication of such phenomena is instructive – they indicate that the assimilation of welfare to the state is not to subject that institution to a moral imperative constructed by welfare philosophers but to the vagaries of the electoral process. It cannot be assumed that the state, through its officials, elected or otherwise, has lower time preferences than individuals. Indeed, the desire for re-election suggests the opposite, with the irresistible implication that governments will inevitably pass on the costs of welfare policies to future generations. There is little theoretical or empirical evidence that the political system is more effective than the market in coping with those inevitable uncertainties in economic and social life that afflict all welfare prospects. Furthermore, there is much which suggests that the steady accretion of the state's welfare responsibilities actually disables it from fulfilling its primary obligation to aid the genuine victims of market society.

VI

There is a depressing implication of almost all welfare theory that it is impossible to conceive of a welfare system that will not have either counterintuitive implications or counterproductive results. Although a complete withdrawal of the state has been recommended by some social theorists, on the ground that insurance and private charity could solve the familiar problems, this is scarcely conceivable. For one thing, if it is utilitarian judgement based on the claim that a purely private system would satisfy individuals' desire for welfare, it is probably empirically false. From the beginning, part of the rationale for public welfare has been that better-off individuals *desire* deprivation-relieving action by public authorities: it is a want logically equivalent to the demand for defence, law and order and all the other familiar activities by the state. That is the kernel of truth that lies at the heart of the public-good theory of welfare and to this extent traditional liberalism is as much a welfarist doctrine as much as any other political ideology.

It could, of course, be countered by an argument, from Nozick, that any welfare (i.e. redistributive) activity by the state involves a violation of individual rights. But this depends upon the demonstration that there are such inviolable rights, and on the dubious claim that, for example, the public provision of defence somehow does not violate them. It should also be remembered that the sudden withdrawal of state welfare would have catastrophic consequences for those people who had 'invested' in it throughout their lives. Indeed, the welfare status quo presents an almost insuperable problem for any liberal subjectivist social theory since it already embodies rights and entitlements. Not only would it be immoral by the conventional welfare philosophy but it would also be condemnable by liberal utilitarianism, which forbids the overriding of preferences in this manner.[18]

Nevertheless, it has to be conceded that the principles of human nature on which early critics of welfare based their arguments have turned out to be depressingly accurate. It seems that there is no system of state welfare, short of the harsh conditions specified in the Poor Laws and echoed faintly in current workfare proposals, which will not have counterproductive effects, either through proving to be too attractive or because of anomalies, such as redistribution to the better off, generated by democratic political

systems. Contemporary experience indicates that far from encouraging a communitarian and socially concerned 'self', the institutions of the welfare state have simply reproduced the traditional
homo economicus in a different context. Furthermore, it is a
context in which the automatic constraints of a market pricing
system are largely absent or at least operate much more slowly
through their political surrogate, the voting mechanism.

Thus, however plausible in an ethical sense the demonstration of
the existence of 'welfare rights' may be, and no matter however
persuasive the case for welfare derived from a theory of citizenship
is, such social philosophies are radically incomplete if they fail to
take account of certain behavioural traits and causal mechanisms
that have been shown to be operative in welfare societies. These
points are recognized by, for example, Raymond Plant in his suggestion that welfare rights should be given constitutional protection
against the vagaries of democratic politics and the activities of the
welfare agencies themselves, and in his recognition that the receipt
of a welfare benefit is not inconsistent with the existence of a corresponding social obligation.[19]

VII

The inference that is to be drawn from the many doubts that have
been raised about the ethics and efficiency of the welfare state in
Western democracies is that the phenomenon of poverty and deprivation is partly a social or cultural problem. It is not caused simply
by a scarcity of resources (although the fragile economic base on
which the assimilation of welfare to the welfare state was founded
is of crucial significance in the disarray of the latter ideal) but by
institutional arrangements which encourage, unwittingly, the per-
petuation of the *malaise* they were designed to alleviate. Thus,
whatever truth there is in propositions about causality in the nineteenth century, it is certainly plausible to suggest that during this
century the direction of causation has, in some cases at least, been
from the complex structure of welfare institutions *to* the reproduc-
tion of welfare problems.

Of crucial importance for the understanding of welfare is an
analysis of two competing and irreconcilable conceptions that were
present in an inchoate way from the very beginning of theorizing
in this area. One restricts notions of well-being to individual,

subjective experiences, the other attributes welfare to 'states of affairs' or aggregate phenomena of a variety of types: a 'welfare improvement' is one that makes society as a whole better off. Although the latter descriptions look as if they are concerned with individualistic experiences, a closer analysis suggests that they are not.The assumption of welfare responsibilities by the state for such wanted goods and services as education, health, pensions, and so on, rests almost always on a highly disputable notion of efficiency, i.e. that the collective provision of them produces an optimal supply. It is said to be consistent with hypothetical individual choices, but will not be generated by private arrangements. However, it has been argued that if all statements of well-being are irredeemably subjective, then the attempt by a central agency (the state) to provide a range of services in the absence of knowledge of people's choices can logically be no other than an imposition of a collective arrangement on what is an unknowable complex of preferences. It is, of course, true that political or collective choice procedures are necessary for the production of a range of goods and services, and that individuals would be worse off (in the subjective sense) in their absence. It is also true that democratic procedures are legitimate surrogates for the market for the satisfaction of people's wants for genuine public goods. However, it is naive to suppose that the continuing process of accretion of welfare functions by the state has led to an increase in well-being. It is this theoretical consideration that lies at the heart of objections to 'bureaucratic welfarism' that emanate from a variety of ideological positions, including socialists ones favourably disposed towards the idea of welfare.

Again, the assimilation of welfare to state welfare is morally questionable even when its rationale is not efficiency, in the welfare economist's sense, but redistributive, in an unalloyed ethical sense. It is here that procedural considerations are paramount too. Irrespective of whether equality of welfare is ethically desirable, or is even a coherent ethical goal, there is no reason to suppose that political choice procedures will generate it. If welfare goods are delivered in kind, then the egalitarian intent that ethically powers them will be distorted and prevented by well-established behavioural assumptions that seem to govern, in the manner of irresistible 'iron laws', the consumption of those services. The middle classes, through that 'beneficial involvement', identified by Le

Grand and Goodin, defy the egalitarian imperative that is implicit in citizenship theory.

The predicaments in the theory and practice of welfare result inexorably from the error of attributing well-being to something other than individual experiences. The recognition of this should result in a normative theory that implies a rejection of end-state or aggregative welfare statements as misconceived and a bias towards the 'selective' delivery of whatever welfare-enhancing policy is deemed to be appropriate for the state. It is the aggregative approach which entails that individuals are mere counters in some social welfare function, rather than autonomous creators of their own futures.

The insistence on welfare as a purely individualistic phenomenon is a feature of classical liberal theorizing since Adam Smith – a feature that was particularly lost in the utilitarian–aggregative mode of reasoning that Benthamites bequeathed to welfare theory, especially to what was to become welfare economics. In the former view, the market was not validated because it maximized some aggregate utility function (a rationale which produced a 'perfectionist' attitude in welfare theorists) but by virtue of its capacity to coordinate the activities of disparate agents pursuing their subjectively-determined goals. It is this that does justice to the demands of autonomy, a value which is such a feature of contemporary state welfare theory. It is that lack of power in individuals to determine their own futures, which welfare state philosophers identified in uncorrected market arrangements, that is so often a consequence of the assumption of the welfare responsibility by the apparatus of the state. This attenuation of autonomy is exemplified both in that policy which distributes welfare independently of social obligations (the form beloved of the crudest of the classical liberals) and in the choice-reducing aspect of 'nationalized' health, housing, education, pensions, and so on. While excluding a repudiation of existing welfare obligations of the state, contemporary individualist theory points in a different direction from the status quo, especially those features that attenuate choice and those that blur and dilute personal responsibility for action. This latter point is alien to almost all socialist welfare theorists, and indeed some cruder classical liberals, who wish to discount the relevance of causal histories to the way in which problems of deprivation are treated. It follows that if the rationale of welfare theory is about autonomy and choice, then welfare policy should be directed towards the many ways in which individuals can be *empowered*, i.e. enabled to make autonomous decisions that enhance their individual well-being. This does not entail that market choice, however necessary, is the only method by which individuals can be empowered. For state involvement can be empowering if it is structured around institutions and policies designed to enhance the well-being of individual citizens rather than those of welfare authorities.

An obvious policy implication of this concept would be the introduction of choice into education by the 'voucher' scheme.[20] In this, parents could theoretically 'spend' their vouchers at schools of their choice, so that the providers of education (teachers and administrators) would be impelled to respond to the consumers wants or face the obvious consequences. There is no reason why the value of the voucher should not be adjusted to income if it were desired that empowering parents also required some egalitarian component. Irrespective of the details of the suggested versions of such schemes, the theoretical element remains constant – that individuals remain the best judges of their own welfare.

This ethical attitude itself is not inconsistent with egalitarianism, although classical liberal subjectivists would have other objections, both theoretical and empirical, to redistribution. However, it is incompatible with any view of welfare that detaches well-being from individual experiences, any normative theory that maintains, either that individuals are not the sole arbiters of their well-being in, say, education or health, or that social policy should transcend individual choice in these areas. Both these latter claims are dependent on their being coherent 'objective' welfare aims and policies. While the concept of welfare may be 'essentially contestable' so that it is just not possible for reason to adjudicate between these rival claims to legitimacy in the usage of concept, the subjectivist perhaps has the edge in the argument, since the 'objectivist' has to show what it is about their preferences that make them qualitatively superior to others. But only the edge, for a fully-fledged subjectivist theory of welfare, takes some courage to sustain. It would have to prohibit *compulsory* health and unemployment insurance, to take two obvious examples. Most theories that take empowerment as the overriding goal of an individualist welfare theory advocate some compulsion to insure in these areas. However, it has to be conceded that the rationale for this partial abridgement of choice, i.e. those who choose not to insure voluntarily might present a welfare problem at a later time, does represent a retreat from subjectivism.

The individualist theory of welfare is not to be interpreted merely as a market theory, in which value is determined by price, for it is quite possible that persons will exercise their choices in such a way that their subjective well-being is advanced in communal action. This is merely to reiterate the point that the welfare debate is not exhausted by the market versus the state dichotomy; it must take account of the variety of social institutions that can emerge through the exercise of freedom. Historically, welfare arrangements have developed spontaneously, mutual aid associations for medical care in the last century being a particularly good example. It is also the case that one of the original functions of British trade unions was to provide welfare benefits for their members.

It is also true that the domain of freedom itself provides a viable opportunity for benevolence. In a modern democratic state the delivery of welfare depends similarly on benevolence – that of the voters. It is therefore at least an open question as to whether the sentiment of benevolence is mobilized more effectively through the political mechanism than by non-political methods. The standard argument in welfare theory is that because welfare has certain public good features, it would not be provided privately; in view of this, the state has the moral authority, as well as the political power, to maximize some (hypothetical) welfare function for society as a whole. However, it has been maintained consistently in this book that, from the subjectivist perspective, it is not possible for this to be known. Conventional assumptions about behaviour in the political process predict that voting reveals people's demands for what are, in effect, private goods supplied by the state. This is, of course, the explanation of the 'capture' of the welfare state by the middle classes. It is this phenomenon that leads to some scepticism about the effectiveness of the political mechanism in the mobilization of the benevolent impulse.

In the light of this, modern welfare theory has shown how it is possible for social cooperation and benevolence to be manifest outside the formal political apparatus: public goods, including the actualization of the welfare sentiment, can be generated spontaneously through reciprocity. It is naive to suppose that, as Titmuss seems to, that the altruistic sentiment itself, unsullied by any suggestion of a corresponding obligation, is sufficient to generate the level of welfare he himself thought desirable, but not at all implausible to suggest that welfare could develop outside both the conventional market and the state. This could occur as long as individuals felt themselves bound morally to cooperate for their mutual advantage. All this means is that voluntary activity between individuals to generate welfare is possible, even though the conventional assumptions of micro-economics imply that the incentive to defect from voluntary agreements is so great that 'free-riding' becomes inevitable. It is claimed, therefore, that any welfare system not backed by coercion becomes highly unstable.

However, it is by no means clear that this is necessarily the case. It is well known that in repeated plays of the 'Prisoners' Dilemma' game, individuals find it in their interests to cooperate. Of course, a person would be much better off from the supply of publicly beneficial activities if he did not contribute to it, but such antisocial behaviour is not inevitable. Certainly in small groups, potential defectors can be 'punished' by cooperators so that they find themselves worse off. As Robert Sugden[21] has shown, what is required for the development of social cooperation is the emergence of the moral property of reciprocity – the rule that one ought to return benefits or favours in the absence of an immediate incentive, provided by either the market or the state. Like other ethical rules, this might emerge by an evolutionary process in which non-cooperators are gradually eliminated through natural selection. It is a process which is much more likely to occur when the supply of socially beneficial activity depends upon everybody's cooperation, i.e. when the advantages of mutuality are readily visible to all. In such circumstances benevolence, which is clearly distinct from altruism, can flourish.

What has all this to do with welfare, as conventionally understood? It is really the germ of a theory which explains how the vicissitudes of life, the misfortunes that afflict people in a sometimes arbitrary manner, and hence generate the demand for state welfare, can be accommodated within an individualist's framework which does not depend on the existence of a naive altruism. Voluntary associations for the solution of welfare problems do not necessarily fall foul of the public-good trap. Indeed, historically, as we have already pointed out, mutual aid associations have developed in this way. Furthermore, an individualistic welfare theory could be constructed out of a combination of private insurance and mutual aid.

However, that such suggestions are at the moment merely speculative is reinforced by the theoretical argument that the feature of 'large numbers' makes this exploitation of the instinct of benevolence and the morality of reciprocity somewhat unlikely. In human associations with large numbers of people, the supply of the benefit does not depend on each person's cooperation; the benefits of cooperation are not immediate so that in such circumstances the threat of mass defection is ever-present. However, this does not mean that the resort to collective welfare by the state is the only alternative: the current dissatisfaction with this from many points on the political spectrum is sufficient to justify a continued scepticism about such a manoeuvre.

One possibility would be to decentralize the welfare function of the state to smaller associations in which the voting mechanism may be more efficient in transmitting the sentiment of benevolence, on which all welfare depends, than it is in national legislatures. It is in these latter institutions that the 'vote motive' produces the collective supply of essentially private goods – the phenomenon that generates both inequality and inattention to the historical aims of welfare policy. It is also the case that smaller political units are a little less vulnerable to the 'knowledge problem' that afflicts all public welfare policies, i.e. the difficulty of obtaining information on welfare preferences in the absence of markets. Finally, the imposition of a reciprocal obligation for the receipt of a welfare benefit, the favoured policy of many citizenship theorists, would be more easily achievable in local political communities than national ones.

All of these tentative suggestions relate to the fundamental proposition that welfare questions are in essence about individual perceptions and attitudes, whether they are mediated through the market, the state or forms of voluntary action that lie outside these two competing domains. It is the attribution of the welfare property to 'social states' or aggregates that has been partially, if not mainly, responsible for the theoretical and practical problems that have become endemic to welfare states since their inception.

Although the welfare rights school, which interprets rights to well-being as claims against the state (and as morally equivalent to rights to forbearance) is formally outside the aggregative tradition, it is characterized by a weakness at the foundational level and an indeterminacy in relation to policy. Are there 'rights' to education and health? If so, how are they to be ordered and is there any principle to decide priorities in the face of scarcity? Again, the vagueness of welfare rights means that there are few theoretical limits on their expansion. It is true that some welfare rights theorists link their recipience with the performance of social obligations. But although this condition may go some way towards solving some of the intractable problems associated with state welfare, it also attenuates their status as genuine entitlements. Thus despite the absoluteness that social theorists wish to associate with welfare rights, the above circumstances make them as prone to the problems associated with the political process as is the more familiar collectivist approach to welfare.

VIII

These considerations suggest that only one thing is clear about the concept of welfare, and that is its seemingly intractable nature. It is apparent in the question of the meaning of the concept itself, and even more so in the area of policy. The complexities have been compounded by the fact that, in the last thirty years, the concept has been inextricably bound up with the philosophy of the welfare state, so that, in some circles at least, the responsibility for the enhancement of well-being is said to rest almost entirely with the state. This has produced a highly disputable social theory that devalues those non-political examples of individual well-being, for example, the satisfactions achieved through voluntary exchange between individuals, that had always been stressed by liberal political economists, amongst others. It also underestimated the importance of non-state institutions for dealing with the dominant welfare problem, the relief of deprivation, and for the supply of typical welfare goods, such as education, health and pensions.

What is also deficient in the philosophy of the welfare state is the inattention paid to the constitutional arrangements for the delivery of welfare. Those theorists who have formulated sophisticated arguments for welfare have rarely enquired into the appropriate procedures for its enactment, or, more important, overlooked the independent effect existing procedures may have on the supply of welfare itself. Yet empirical investigations suggest strongly that democratic institutions not only generate welfare almost autonomously but also produce perverse effects, especially when the good is delivered non-selectively and in the form of specified services. Historically, there has been an implicit assumption that ideal forms of state welfare would be constructed by benevolent rulers immune from the normal motivations of political actors; or that political leaders of all persuasions would be permeated, in a Fabian-like manner, with certain welfare ideals. All this, however, presupposed an agreement about social ends which is unlikely to exist in pluralistic societies (although there is some evidence of a short-lived welfare consensus in Western democracies during the first decades after the end of the Second World War). In the absence of this, the welfare issue is certain to be subject to often unpredictable movements of political opinion and electoral pressure.

It is, of course, impossible to take welfare out of politics but future debate about the subject is likely to focus as much on constitutional questions as on substantive ethical ones. Political theorists should therefore pay more attention to the procedures for transmitting the subjective choices that people have for state welfare more *efficiently* than the prevailing methods. Although it is fanciful to suppose that there will be substantial changes in the welfare systems in Britain or the USA, the growing recognition that wellbeing is an individual phenomenon which is not necessarily advanced by a state apparatus that is as sensitive to electoral pressure as it is to the demands of a rational welfare ethic, indicates that the times are propitious for a fundamental re-examination of the whole issue. The return of education, health, pensions, and so on, to individuals through various methods of empowerment, such as the voucher scheme, could, in principle, mark the beginnings of a new consensus. The decentralization of welfare services to smaller political units would be a more feasible way of advancing the moral claims and the attendant social obligations associated with communitarian and citizenship theories than is the method of national legislation. Again, the re-activation of a genuine insurance principle for such things as retirement pensions would prevent the burdening of future generations with debt.

None of this, however, is likely to happen. The subject of welfare remains intractable both at the theoretical level and in the area of public policy. Despite the resurgence of a more individualistic approach to public affairs, and an acceptance by many writers that well-being is a subjective phenomenon, there is no consensus on this. To many theorists, individuals do have needs that are independent of their desires, and indeed it is claimed *pari passu* that a society does have ends which are not reducible to individual choices. It is this claim which justifies the assimilation of welfare to the welfare state, and hence the inevitable paternalism that accompanies that form of social organization. This dichotomy, between individualism and collectivism, this apparently unbridgeable gulf between the potential ethical nihilism of subjectivism and the prospective authoritarianism of objectivism, in theorizing about welfare, is but a special case of the larger division within social and political theory as a whole. It is a fundamental dispute that is hardly likely to be settled by minor reforms of welfare institutions.

8

Welfare:
A Postscript

There have been many changes in the political and intellectual worlds since this book was first published in 1990. Most noticeable, of course, has been the demise of the socialist dream of a rationally-planned society without markets. The most spectacular example of the defeat of this project was the collapse of communism but an equally significant case was the rethinking of the welfare system that has occurred in most Western democracies. Some of the conceptual apparatus that has been used in this re-orientation of social thinking was discussed in Chapter 7 of the first edition of this book but the penetration of the welfare debate by pro-market and individualistic thinking that has occurred is remarkable. Almost all conventional welfare states are now experimenting with welfare reforms and some of the innovations have come from nominally socialist governments. Still, the collectivist social insurance state remains intact, despite its escalating cost, in all countries where it has been long established. The second sort of state welfare discussed in the first edition, that redistribution of income aimed at the relief of poverty, has again survived the intellectual onslaught from conservative social theorists who have sedulously chronicled the dysfunctional social behaviour it seems to produce.

Despite the successful revival of conservative and economic liberal ideas about welfare, the familiar conceptual categories remain. Thus the claims of an individualist approach to welfare policy, which would entail the privatization of whole segments of the welfare state, are resisted by those who deny that welfare is exhausted by the experience of personal well-being. For the latter, the whole idea of welfare is inextricably bound up with the values of community. The collectivist impulse may not seek wholesale nationalization of the economy but its advocates feel that certain aspects of social life should not be left to the vagaries of the market. These social purposes would include the production of typical welfare goods such as unemployment insurance, healthcare, education and pensions, as well as poverty relief.

The most frequently cited principle used to validate an extensive role for the state in these areas is *need*. An analysis of this concept still reveals the differences that divide contemporary welfare thinkers. The major rationale for the welfare state is that its institutions and policies meet with needs, about which it is assumed that there is a possibility of agreement amongst well-disposed analysts. The demonstration of an objective need in a person creates a prima facie obligation on some other agent or institution to satisfy it. This may be theoretically equivalent to the obligation to protect people from aggressive and invasive conduct. The meeting of genuine need may not be the only purpose of the welfare state but it is presumed to be its major one.

The claims for need derive largely from a suggested distinction between needs and wants (or mere preferences). The market takes care of wants, and the satisfaction of them will undeniably depend on income; their origin lies deep in personal psychology and certainly they are subjective and vary according to whim. We decide to have certain preferences or wants rather than find ourselves with them, as is the case with the need for healthcare or food. Of course, many of the wants expressed in modern society are not needed in any urgent or pressing sense. They have no a priori claim to satisfaction.

Needs, however, are thought to be objective in that their existence is not a function of the psychology of the individual. Needs are facts about persons and have the aura of determinacy; a person cannot help but have them. They may even be capable of scientific demonstration. David Wiggins claims that: 'What I need depends not on thought or the workings of my mind (or not only on these) but on the way the world is.'[1] The existence of a need depends not at all on a person's awareness of it – indeed, one may not want what is needed just as one may often not need what is wanted (no matter how intensively the want is felt). It follows that other people may have a better understanding of needs than particular agents precisely because they are thought to be objective. Only the welfare state can satisfy these needs, and theoretically the demands of the needy (even if not expressed) must be met even if persons lack income.

In modern welfare states, however, many things which might be thought to be wants, even if of an important kind, are presented as needs requiring collective provision. Thus George and Wilding argue that: 'The fundamental principle of radical social policy is that resources, whether in the field of health, education, housing or income, should be distributed according to need.'[2] But it is an illusion to suppose that the so-called objectivity of need can morally authorize the state to make the major object of social policy its satisfaction. Even the plausible candidates listed by George and Wilding, such as education and health, have an irreducible shade of subjectivism about them. Just how much education or health is to be provided is a matter of choice, expressed either through the ballot box or in the marketplace. If medical needs were truly objective then there would be no dispute about resource allocation in a nationalized health service: some agency would know just how much to spend on hip replacements, cardiac surgery, cancer treatment, etc. But apart from obvious needs in an emergency, health-care expenditure has to be to an extent subjective, and subject to rationing, either by price or by administrative fiat. And the same reasoning applies to education, for while there might be agreement about the needs for literacy and numeracy, there are obvious disputes about expenditure above basic levels. Should higher education, which will guarantee the consumer a highly paid job, be provided at zero price because it is an objective need?

Indeed, the objectivity of need may be challenged, and hence the claim that it provides an incorrigible justification for the collectivized welfare state doubted. Although in some instances a need looks as if it is not chosen, this is by no means obviously so. Most need are translatable into wants. I may appear to need medical treatment but this is because I want to live a life of a certain quality. Beyond a certain point, medical treatment, since it is subject to scarcity, rests ultimately on subjective choice; decisions have to be made about potentially competing ends. We can assume that people want to survive, so what appears to be an objective need is in reality a want of particular intensity and urgency. Also, someone may not want to live if that means enduring pain, and the decision there must obviously be a subjective one.

Needs are not physical things out there waiting to be identified by a competent observer but are intimately related to plans and purposes, and these are subjectively chosen. That there are problems about priorities among competing needs itself undermines the claim that they are objective and indubitable. In Western societies, which are especially valued for their moral *pluralism*, there is thought to be something of a conceit about the suggestion that some agency can know how to rank needs according to their urgency. Indeed, the claim that needs are objective and distinct from intensively felt wants sounds paternalistic, as much of the welfare state's activity technically is. Allied to this point is the powerful argument that there is a relativism about needs, for what is now thought to be a needed welfare good in the West would be thought to be a luxury in poorer countries. Finally, even if there were objective needs, it does not logically follow that there is a duty on the state to meet them; in welfare history, there has been a variety of voluntary agencies whose members regarded it as their moral duty to care for people in distress.

None of this precludes the case for state welfare but it casts serious doubt on the objectivity of need arguments that are traditionally mounted in its defence. Indeed, the modern welfare state is by no means limited to the satisfaction of needs and this is admitted by its defenders. Social insurance is cited as an overriding priority as is the claim that there is a duty on the state to 'smooth out' earnings over a lifetime. Furthermore, many of the redistributions of the welfare state, in cash and in kind, have little to with the satisfaction of objective need. Need is used rhetorically in welfare arguments, often as a disguise for the ultimately subjective arguments that take place about public policy.

Rival conceptions of the welfare state

What has emerged in welfare argument today is a serious debate about two rival views of the state's responsibility. They have been summarized as the 'residual' and the 'institutional' welfare states. They are both redistributive, though in subtly different ways, and they have both generated serious policy problems which have vexed social theorists and governments – though the problems have remarkably different philosophical bases and divergent theories of human behaviour.

The residual welfare state may even be called the Poor Law system, for its concern is solely with the elimination of deprivation – which can secure considerable agreement (even the rich do feel worse off if eliminable poverty exists). The meaning of welfare is limited to the increase in well-being that is a product of some (minimal) redistribution from the rich to the very poor. It has little to do with any advancement of community interests that might occur because of the universal provision of particular welfare services. In its purest form, the redistribution is in the form of cash with no conditions attached to the use of that income. This form of welfare is a feature of the USA and, to a lesser extent, Britain, although both these countries have welfare that goes beyond cash redistribution. One feature of this welfare is its reliance on means-testing, which it has to use if the aim of the residual welfare state is to be achieved.

The rival to this form of welfare is the *institutional* welfare state which involves everyone in the community in the consumption of welfare goods, e.g. healthcare, unemployment insurance, pensions, education, and so on. The theoretical underpinnings for the institutional welfare state derive partly from the system of mutual insurance that it provides and partly from the value of social solidarity that is supposed to flow from the common consumption of welfare goods and services. This is thought to produce a different kind of moral agent: not that abstract utility-maximizer of classical liberal social theory who is separated from their fellow citizens, but a cooperative, less individualistic person capable of taking on the burdens of citizenship and conducting relationships of reciprocity with other members of an inclusive community. Their welfare is not exclusively a function of their income but also comprises that communal well-being which universal services apparently produce.

There is a form of redistribution in the institutional welfare state but it is not from rich to poor via cash payments but is a series of transfers within particular groups, for example, from the healthy to the sick through a universal health service which is free at the point of consumption, from the employed to the temporarily idle and from the young to the old through a pension based on an inter-generational contract.[3] There is perhaps an unstable mixture of quasi-insurance principles and communitarian values here but it is a common welfare goal. One advantage of it is that the more people that are covered by these arrangements, the less reliance there is on means-testing, with the affronts to personal dignity that they involve. A clear difference between the European and the British welfare states can be detected in this issue, for the former have a more inclusive set of social arrangements which precludes the segregation of people according to income. The survival of these quite costly schemes in Europe may well be a consequence of the anti-individualism there.

It is in the analyses of these types of public welfare that the most innovative contributions to welfare theory and practice have been generated. Each has disadvantages that go to the heart of welfare theory. The problem with the residual welfare state is the dysfunctional behaviour it might encourage; that with the institutional welfare state is not merely its excessive costs but also the threat to liberty and choice that the collective delivery of welfare involves.

The welfare state and the relief of deprivation

However need is defined, the primary aim of the welfare state is the relief of poverty. In the USA, the *meaning* of welfare seems to be restricted to those arrangements which have been made to take care of the deprived. The concept does not apply to other welfare schemes, such as social security; the recipients of that are assumed to have paid for it, even though in actuarial terms they have not. The rationale for the minimalist welfare state is the relief of deprivation, but it is difficult to specify with any real precision what the precise obligations are here. What also has become more important over recent years is the extent to which personal responsibility should be taken into account in the analysis of deprivation, and in the policy prescriptions that are aimed at its relief. For some writers, the very fact that people are in a distressed state is a sufficient reason for directing aid towards them. In this 'snapshot' view of the world, the existence of suffering is the only thing that matters and it should be relieved, without question.[4] For others, who take a more long-term and causal view of the occurrence of social distress, how things come about is important. People may get into difficulties through wilful behaviour and any relief of their predicament should be so designed that it does not encourage others to behave in a similar manner. Welfare policy should guard against moral hazard (see Chapter 4). The problem of unmarried motherhood is the most obvious contemporary example of this. However, the difficulty with any welfare policy that tries to overcome moral hazard is that it punishes the deserving poor; this has been known since the Poor Law. All the innovations in the theoretical analysis of this form of welfare have come from the USA. This might be because this is the way that welfare is understood in that country and it is there that the most research has been done on the social consequences of a primarily cash-based poverty relief system. The main debate concerns the effectiveness of the ameliorative measures that have been taken in the past thirty years in social democracies. There have been serious doubts at the practical level as to whether they have achieved the welfare goal of integrating people into the community and, ultimately, reducing the numbers of those on welfare. There has been a remarkable rise in the numbers on means-tested benefits in Britain and the USA which has opened an intense debate about the purposes of social welfare. Welfare may have originally been directed at the working poor, normally in a household headed by a male, low-paid earner, but it is now increasingly the resort of the victims of family breakdown, unmarried mothers who have never worked and others who constitute a dependency culture which is reproduced through the generations.

In the first edition of this book, some attention (Chapter 7) was devoted to the criticism that had emerged of the Great Society programmes in the USA. These were programmes specifically designed to deal with the poverty problem in that country. Some conservative and classical liberal theorists had then claimed that the poverty problem had not been solved despite the expenditure but had actually worsened (though the share of such programmes as a proportion of government spending is low[5]). The numbers officially poor had not been reduced and, worse, family breakdown had intensified, especially in the black community, and the inner-city areas had declined into ghettoes of poverty, crime and drug addiction. Easily obtainable welfare was producing a dysfunctional underclass. There were two serious responses, one relying on the behavioural assumptions of orthodox social science, i.e. people respond to incentives and the welfare provisions had produced moral hazard. People may have wanted to work and to form stable families but the system produced a conflict between what is the right thing to do and what is the (technically) rational course of action. In Charles Murray's analysis, which he has continued since the publication of his *Losing Ground*[6] in 1984, people respond to signals and although he is concerned with morality, he does not think that moral education can compete successfully with the opportunities for indolence and dysfunctional behaviour provided by welfare. And as a libertarian[7] he does not want to vest government with the powers to provide such an education. His claim is that small government will spontaneously generate morality and good behaviour. The most important problem that is facing the American welfare system is the rise in illegitimacy and the decline in the conventional two-parent family. Just to what extent this is causally determined by the welfare system or is a product of cultural changes it is difficult to say. It might not be significantly reduced even if all incentives to unmarried motherhood were removed.

A slightly different conservative critique comes from the work of Lawrence Mead, whose early work, *Beyond Entitlement*, was briefly discussed in the first edition of this book. In this and his later work, *The New Politics of Poverty*,[8] he has produced just as powerful a critique of American public welfare as Murray, but its normative bite does not derive from the premise of small government. Indeed, Mead's analysis subverts the classical liberal's and the conservative's critique of welfare by arguing that social dysfunctioning can only be prevented in a welfare world that reduces personal liberty and which authorizes the state to play quite an active role in educating and training people for civil society. They must be made competent and able to cope with the difficulties and responsibilities of the workplace. He claims that 'the solution to the work problem lies not in freedom but in governance'.[9] Obviously, the very worst nostrum to the poverty problem for Mead would be any form of negative income tax or guaranteed wage, something which Murray[10] now seems to accept, in a modified form, despite being an early critic of it.

Mead's point is that the welfare state has produced a new form of poverty – confined largely to those who do not work and are never likely to work. Whereas originally welfare schemes were designed to act as a supplement to the incomes of the working poor, they now provide a permanent (though not a very comfortable) way of life to millions of single female-headed households in the USA. His claim is that they are more or less impervious to policy changes recommended by classical liberal analysts. Mead's favourite example here is the fact that unmarried motherhood did not vary when a reduction in the value of benefits occurred in the late 1970s. A lot of pro-welfare state writers have used this fact to reject the economistic and causal approach to the explanation of welfare dependency. But the latter argument does not depend solely on the effect of income changes on behaviour. It has been noticed that although the cash value of the benefits fell in the USA, other factors, such as the relaxation of the conditions for qualifying for benefits were equally important in the causation of dependency. The whole package of incentives still made it worthwhile being a single, unemployed mother.[11]

Mead's argument is that work must be *enforced*; the receipt of welfare should be conditional on work, either in the private sector or in government schemes. Indeed, his ideas have had a more direct influence on American policy than have those of more orthodox economic conservative theorists (and certainly they appear more politically marketable than economic liberal doctrines which have historically tried to combine some welfare provision with personal freedom). Workfare has been a part of various American welfare schemes for some time – the country's federal system allows individual states some latitude to experiment and some did introduce forms of workfare. But because the federal government has always been heavily involved in the financing of welfare, the possibilities were limited.

A real inhibition to root and branch reform of the welfare system was the existence of a particular federal entitlement – Aid to Families with Dependent Children (AFDC). This had originally been a welfare programme (dating from the New Deal) designed to assist the children of deprived mothers (widows and divorcees) but its provisions were extended after 1950 and it became the major source of income for mothers of illegitimate children. Out of wedlock births soared from 5 per cent in 1960 to 28 per cent in 1990 (68 per cent in the black community). The poor in the USA are mainly those on welfare (35 per cent are female heads of families) and only 2 per cent of those in work are poor. The welfare state has virtually ceased to have anything to do with the traditional working class and this phenomenon introduced a new type of politics that was impossible to identify as Democratic or Republican, progressive or conservative. The new issues are the behavioural problems associated with this form of welfare. Theoretically at least, the response to these problems brought about a new concept of citizenship, one that stresses the duties that are owed to society by the recipients of welfare, not their unabridged rights to that income. It is a theory that gradually attracted politicians and attempts were made by the federal government to reform welfare in the direction of workfare, first in 1988 with the Family Support Act and later in the much more radical Personal Responsibility and Work Opportunity Reconciliation Act (PRWORA) passed in 1996. The problem with previous experiments with workfare was that it was not enforced and AFDC normally exempted unmarried mothers from a work obligation. PRWORA transfers welfare responsibility from the federal government to the states, who receive block grants to spend as they wish, subject to conditions which prevent the restoration of the old system. Thus PRWORA removes the formal federal entitlement of AFDC, and although it continues in a modified form through the Temporary Assistance to Needy Families programme, there is a time limit (two years) to welfare recipients and, in theory, there are onerous work and training obligations.

It is too early to say how all this will work out, but there are encouraging signs, especially from states like Wisconsin which had already introduced workfare programmes before they became obligatory. But orthodox conservatives who adopt some version of the economic determinist approach are sceptical; they maintain that as long as some incentives not to work remain they will be decisive influences on behaviour. They also doubt whether any government really has the will to enforce workfare. Charles Murray argues that workfare schemes have only worked in the past for people who would have worked anyway.

Still, what Mead's argument reveals is a new approach to citizenship. As he points out,[12] implicit in the T.H. Marshall view of citizenship (see Chapter 5) was an implicit theory of *reciprocity*, i.e. recipients of welfare owed society something in return. However, the Marshallian concept of welfare rights was interpreted differently by later welfare writers: welfare was seen as a right to which people were entitled regardless of their conduct. In Mead's view, the form in which welfare has been traditionally delivered in the USA has prevented the development of a proper notion of citizenship. Indeed, liberals (in the American sense) regard some people as incompetent, and incapable of achieving competence; that is why they persistently oppose workfare schemes.

A serious argument against both the Charles Murray and Lawrence Mead critiques of American welfare policy has been mounted by William Julius Wilson[13] and it centres on the causation of welfare problems through the unavailability of work. His argument is important because it does not depend on the familiar explanation for the plight of the underclass and the disadvantages of minorities (especially the black population) in the USA in terms of discrimination. He has provoked the ire of the conventional welfare school by arguing that federal action and judicial decision making in the USA has eliminated most of the serious impediments to work which once existed through racial bias. His explanation of the inner-city problem is that there has been a dramatic reduction in employment opportunities for disadvantaged people. The old manufacturing jobs that used to be located in the inner cities have largely disappeared. They have been replaced by new high-tech industries that are situated in the suburbs and which demand skills the people do not have. There is a mismatch between the type of work available and the qualities of potential employees. Furthermore, the type of persons who relocate in the suburbs to find the new jobs are just the sort of people who should be examples of civility. The people who now remain in the inner city are likely to be on welfare and part of the drug and criminal culture.

The emergence of the underclass has little to do with welfare. For Wilson, the line of causation runs from the unavailability of work, through to welfare dependency and dysfunctional behaviour, whereas for the conservatives the link is more or less directly from the institutions of welfare to social disorder (even if they disagree about the exact pattern of causality). For Wilson, it would follow that a more old-fashioned interventionist approach is the answer to the welfare problem. This might require direct job creation by government or more active macro-economic policy to tackle directly the type of unemployment created in the modern economy.

Welfare theorists agree that there might be something to all this but deny that it is the sole, or even the major, cause of the welfare problems that afflict the inner cities in the USA. In fact, historically, American labour has been very mobile; in previous periods of economic restructuring people moved to where the jobs were. This is, of course, true of the black population which in the past was prepared to move long distances in search of employment. Also, the critical point is now made that much of the relocation of American industry was brought about *because* the inner cities had become crime infested and their populations incompetent in Mead's sense.

It is important to note that, in comparison to Europe, the USA has a great capacity to create jobs. Although the jobs may be unattractive, people tend not to stay in them for long but move quickly up the income scale once they acquire the habits of work. Indeed, one of the major claims of American welfare theorists is that a job, no matter how badly paid, is itself an education in civility and citizenship.

The view that welfare problems emerge because of the unavailability of work looks a little more plausible in relation to Britain and Europe than in the USA. In British welfare theory, the Beveridge social insurance system was normally seen in the context of a full-employment policy generated by Keynesian demand management economic strategy (see Chapter 3). That is why the institutional welfare state took the form that it did – a system of temporary relief for people who would normally be in full employment. But the nature of the welfare system has changed. It is now as much addressed to recipients of means-tested benefits, unmarried mothers and victims of family breakdown. But compared to the USA, job opportunities are harder to come by in Britain. Also the welfare system which makes employment less attractive because of 'poverty traps' and means-testing produces many undesirable consequences, most notably a reduced incentive to work since people lose their benefits if they earn too much. Furthermore, it encourages fraud.

Yet the abolition of means-testing and the granting of universal benefits produces its own anomalies, the most spectacular being the fact that, under universalism, aid goes to those who do not need it, at least by the definition of 'need' described earlier. There is a justification for universalism which derives from the communitarian element in welfare theory: this understands people as citizens and entitled to certain collective advantages of communal living. To make the receipt of such income a matter of discrimination according to means apparently creates a certain divisiveness: a society is marked out into the providers of welfare (the taxpayers) and the grateful beneficiaries. But it is doubtful whether institutions of the welfare state and its universal benefits produce that communal spirit which for which theorists had hoped.

In fact, the providers normally resent having to pay for people whom they regard as often the *undeserving* poor. They reject the imposition onto the taxpayer of the problems that individuals find themselves in. And some welfare problems are a consequence of people mismanaging their lives. Hence in European welfare states, the better off are anxious to retain certain highly questionable welfare advantages, such as universal Child Benefit.

The institutional welfare state

The difficulties of the welfare state arise partly out of the fact that the underlying moral and political justification for its existence is confused. It is seen by some to be an essential protection for individuals against poverty and the vicissitudes of economic life. Misfortunes can afflict anyone and as citizens we owe each other a generalized duty of care. However, the welfare state also provides services which are not directed at the poor but are enjoyed by everyone (subject to their meeting certain not very demanding requirements) and which in some cases, if not all, could be provided by the market or which were historically delivered by voluntary associations. The services of the institutional welfare state cover healthcare, education, pensions, unemployment protection and other facilities which, superficially at least, have little to do with 'objective need'.

The ultimate rationale for state-supplied compulsory insurance remains the same. The state is stepping in to supply public goods in the face of market failure, although there has never been agreement amongst economists as to whether there is genuine market failure in health, pensions and unemployment insurance. One feature which is used to justify state provision, not mentioned in the first edition of this book, is the phenomenon of 'adverse selection'. In certain private insurance markets, those most likely to be afflicted with a calamity, like ill-health or unemployment, are those most likely to insure against it. The insurance companies cannot pick out in advance who those people are and therefore highly unstable markets are produced with potentially ruinously high premiums. The element of compulsion in state schemes spreads the risk, and also helps cope with the problem of 'co-variance', where misfortunes interact on the grand scale, such as in a serious economic depression. Private insurance is unable to cope with widespread catastrophe.

However, in recent years, there have been some theoretical[14] (and practical) attempts to remedy these problems. Even the hitherto intractable problem of unemployment insurance might be solved by market methods. In the early history of capitalism, the earnings of labour were probably too low to finance widespread unemployment insurance but as a society gets richer the returns to labour gradually catch up with those of capital. In a private insurance market, the system could be self-financing. Insurance companies would monitor the working of the system so as to avoid moral hazard and competition would produce manageable premiums and benefits. Most important, private insurance companies would not provide unemployment pay indefinitely, which is the bane of state schemes. In a private world, there would be every incentive for recipients of unemployment pay to seek work since the commitment to pay benefits would not be open-ended.

It is undoubtedly the cost, and perceived less than satisfactory quality, of social insurance-based welfare that is causing a serious re-examination of the ways of supplying the typical welfare goods. In all social democratic countries, the costs of state welfare have risen seemingly inexorably and are more or less impervious to changes in general economic fortunes. Although it has been calculated[15] that to preserve the present welfare system in Britain over the next few decades would require government to spend only an additional 5 per cent of gross domestic product (GDP) on the services, that would itself involve a considerable increase in the tax burden. It would produce significant tax resistance. Social surveys often indicate that taxpayers are willing to pay for extra spending on education and health, but they answer such questions in the absence of choices about alternatives and without the actual experience of paying the additional costs. When they go to the polls they tend to punish political parties that threaten to increase taxes for general welfare spending. An equally important point is that, in social democratic countries, the electoral system is inefficient at transmitting people's desires for valued public welfare goods, especially health and education. This is why people 'exit' and buy them privately.

The real crisis in welfare states is likely to arise from the political granting of guarantees which cannot be honoured. The classic example here is state pensions that are delivered by a Pay As You Go (PAYG) arrangement; under this, one generation of young workers pays for the current retired generation on the assumption that the next generation will honour the promise. This quasi-contractual model of pension provision compares unfavourably to systems which are fully funded on the stock market. The latter are less vulnerable to demographic changes such as the decline in the birthrates of advanced Western democracies which are making their PAYG pension systems unsustainable. But the great invest-ment of the private pension funds leads to a deepening of the capital structure of an economy so that output can be sustained with a declining workforce. Britain's pension problem is less severe than those of other European Union countries since the country has more people[16] in private schemes (in addition to the basic state pension, which is of very low value). There is an earnings-related state pension which remains for people who do not belong to private occupational schemes. Still, because of arrangements like this, the welfare system in Britain is not facing the same crisis as in more statist countries.

Almost all state pensions schemes start out, like Beveridge's, with the aim of being funded, so that they are not technically redis-tributive welfare, but this is never achieved. Although reforms in the American system under Reagan were designed to build up 'trust' funds to relieve the burden on future generations, actual pension contributions were used to fund public spending so that the trusts' finances now consist of government debt which will one day have to be redeemed if the pensions promise is to be honoured. This will prove extremely costly; indeed, most young Americans assume that they will not receive Social Security (or at least not at the level of their parents) when they retire.

In addition to these obvious problems, a further anomalous feature of state pension schemes is beginning to attract the atten-tion of welfare theorists: this is the implicit inequality built into state schemes. If they are earnings related, the inequalities of working life are simply reproduced in old age. There is nothing at all wrong with this in funded arrangements because the higher pay-ments in them are a product of higher savings by particular persons; but since PAYG schemes are unfunded they are more like welfare arrangements than proper insurance. However, an equally contro-versial inequality which occurs in the USA is that between the races. On average, whites live longer than blacks so that young black workers are supporting better-off white people in their old age.[17] Of course, there has always been the anomaly of the position of women in state pension systems; they retire earlier and normally have a significantly greater life expectancy. All these may be less obvious examples of inequity than that between the generations, but they will attract more attention as PAYG pensions plans mature. The inequalities produced here follow the same logic of the perverse redistribution to the better off produced by state welfare; they have been examined in Chapter 6.

Existing examples of privatized pension schemes have shown that it is perfectly feasible to introduce them. Chile[18] in the 1980s successfully moved from an entirely state system to a funded one. Although saving for old age is compulsory, citizens have considerable freedom (though it is not unrestricted) in their choice of investments. The Central Provident Fund in Singapore has produced a type of funding arrangement, although it is much more centrally directed than the Chilean system. The necessity for some compulsion in these arrangements, so that the familiar problems, e.g. moral hazard, described by welfare theorists can be solved, is still consistent with considerable freedom of choice. The only difficulty would appear to occur in the privatization of mature PAYG schemes since one generation will have to pay twice, for the current retirees and for their own old age.

The future of welfare

A strong implication of the first edition of this book, reinforced in these final thoughts, was that the mid-twentieth-century association of welfare with state welfare was mistaken. At the conceptual level it is the case that the sources of well-being arc varied; they can come from voluntary organizations, churches and so on, as well as from the market itself. The state is a comparative latecomer here and in its early involvement with poverty it did not concern itself with the intricacies of people's welfare hopes and ideals; it did not provide healthcare, education or pensions, for example.

There is an epistemological issue here: according to early critics of state welfare, no central organization could have the knowledge of people's welfare goals, or of the many ways of achieving them. All of this information was locked in the interstices of civil society and best coordinated by local, individual and other types of uncoerced action. The state should perhaps confine itself to the relief of obvious cases of deprivation. It should also be constantly on guard against moral hazard, which the designers of the 1834 Poor Law were, although in a somewhat exaggerated way.

It is because many of the welfare problems of the modern world seem to be a product of state action, that many theorists have looked towards less compulsory and coercive methods of achieving welfare. This new emphasis on localism and voluntarism covers both the basic demands of welfare *and* the provision of the 'higher' welfare goods, such as education and healthcare.

In a sombre comment on the American welfare system, Nathan Glazer writes: 'every piece of social policy substitutes for some traditional arrangement ... in which public authorities take over, at least in part, the role of the family, the ethnic and neighbourhood group, of voluntary associations'.[19] It is also argued that the natural compassion of Americans towards the poor was perverted when, from the anti-Depression strategies of the 1930s to the Great Society reforms of the 1960s, the state became responsible for almost every aspect of their well-being. That reciprocity between the giver and the beneficiary of welfare withered when the state became the sole provider. The egoism of the market was transmitted to the public realm so that welfare recipients owed no obligations in return for their aid.[20]

A significant argument in favour of voluntarism and localism is the fact that they make moral hazard easier to overcome; decentralized agents delivering welfare are more likely to have knowledge of the circumstances in which welfare problems arise and be more alert to abuses of the system. This consideration would apply whether the welfare is delivered privately or publicly.

There is now a vast body of historical evidence which shows that welfare schemes covering sickness, unemployment and old age were in place before the advent of social insurance in the twentieth century. Before the Liberal Government's 1911 social insurance legislation there was a myriad of friendly societies and other voluntary organizations[21] to which the bulk of the population belonged. There was no compulsion, which many theorists think is necessary to overcome the adverse selection problem, yet coverage was widespread. What is remarkable is that the phenomenon of friendly societies (and trade union-based welfare organizations) seems to have been common to all Western societies. The USA had a thriving network of friendly societies before it was effectively emasculated by compulsory state welfare (as occurred in Germany and Britain). What is also interesting is the fact that the professional

medical associations in Britain and the USA[22] were active in promoting government-decreed health standards because they feared
being undercut by the more economical services provided by the
friendly societies.

At the conceptual level, debate about the nature of welfare will
continue with the same intensity: it is an argument that is persistently
conducted in the somewhat outdated categories of individualism and
collectivism. They are misleading since collectivism has come to
mean state direction whereas some collective action to solve welfare
problems is voluntary and has a long history. Welfare costs are exter-
nalized, but not onto the general taxpayer. Such activities are
examples of genuine communitarianism since they derive exclusively from spontaneous action by discrete groups and social
organizations. All too often communitarianism is presented as a doctrine that is antithetical to private initiatives (in welfare theory that
normally means opposition to private insurance) and is unduly sup-
portive of the common consumption of compulsory state schemes.
In the welfare world of the future, expanded genuine private insurance arrangements, in conjunction with voluntary organizations,
might well compete with the hitherto dominant welfare state.

In Britain, the welfare debate is likely to be about the problems
associated with the rise of means-tested benefits. They have con-
tributed much to the current welfare problem and are almost certain
to do so more in the future. They produce poverty traps in that the
loss of benefits consequent on moving from unemployment to work
will continue to be a considerable disincentive to work. They also
offer great temptations to fraud. Although Britain has not generated
the problem of a growing and almost permanent 'underclass'
equivalent to that which is only just being tackled in America, there
are signs that the country is moving in that direction. In both cases
welfare is less about temporary aid to the deprived and more about
the provision of a permanent way of life to what has become a segre-
gated category of people. A proposed remedy, such as a guaranteed
minimum income and the reintegration of people into the national
insurance system, is likely to be too costly, in the short-run at least.
Any 'rational' solution to the welfare problem seems to run up
against insuperable problems which seem to have their origin in
human nature.

Notes

Chapter 1

1 N.P. Barry, *The New Right* (London: Croom Helm, 1987); D. Green, *The New Right* (Brighton, London: Wheatsheaf, 1987).
2 D. Bell, *The End of Ideology* (New York: The Free Press, 1962).
3 T.H. Green, *Principles of Political Obligation*, in R. Nettleship (ed.), *Green's Works* (London: Longman, 1881).
4 Sir Henry Maine, *Ancient Law* (London: Murray, 1890), p. 170.
5 Adam Smith, *The Theory of Moral Sentiments*, D.D. Raphael and A. Macfie (eds) (Oxford: Clarendon Press, 1976).
6 Quoted in R. Nisbet, *Conservatism* (Milton Keynes: Open University Press, 1986), p. 37. See also *Thoughts and Details on Scarcity*, Volume 7 of Edmund Burke's *Works* (London: Rivington, 1815–27).
7 See J. Griffin, *Well-being* (Oxford: Clarendon Press, 1986).
8 F. Edgeworth, *Papers Relating to Political Economy* (London: Macmillan, 1925), Vol. III.
9 J. Le Grand, *The Strategy of Equality* (London: Allen and Unwin, 1982).
10 R.M. Titmuss, *The Gift Relationship* (London: Allen and Unwin, 1970).
11 R.H. Tawney, 'Social democracy in Britain', in R. Hinden (ed.) *The Radical Tradition* (Harmondsworth: Penguin, 1966), p. 172.
12 K. Marx, *Early Texts* (Oxford: Blackwell, 1972). It should be stressed that most contemporary communitarians are not Marxists.
13 Quoted in J. Clarke, A. Cochrane and Carol Smart (eds), *Ideologies of Welfare* (London: Hutchinson, 1987), p. 46.

Chapter 2

1 B. Mandeville, *The Fable of the Bees*, F.B. Kaye (ed.) (London: Oxford University Press, 1924). First published 1705.
2 Adam Smith, *The Theory of Moral Sentiments*, D.D. Raphael and A.

Macfie (eds) (Oxford: Clarendon Press, 1976), p. 82. First published 1759.

3 Ibid., p. 263.

4 'There is no art which one government sooner learns from another than that of draining money from the people's pockets', Adam Smith, *An Enquiry into the Nature and Causes of the Wealth of Nations*, R.H. Campbell, A.S. Skinner and W.B. Todd (eds) (London: Oxford University Press, 1976), p. 861. First published 1776.

5 Ibid., p. 456.

6 Ibid., p. 624.

7 B. Mandeville, *The Fable of the Bees*, Vol. 1, p. 169.

8 *The Wealth of Nations*, op. cit., p. 788.

9 Ibid., p. 723.

10 J. Bentham, *An Introduction to the Principles of Morals and Legislation*, J.H. Burns and H.L.A. Hart (eds) (London: Athlone Press, 1982), p. 11.

11 See W. Stark, *Bentham's Economic Writings* (London: Allen and Unwin, 1952–54).

12 J. Bentham, *A Constitutional Code*, F. Rosen and J.H. Burns (eds) (London: Oxford University Press, 1983).

13 See S.E. Finer, *The Life and Times of Edwin Chadwick* (London: Oxford University Press, 1952).

14 See D. Fraser, *The Evolution of the British Welfare State* (London: Macmillan, 1973).

15 See M. Blaug, 'The Myth of the Old Poor Law and the Making of the New', *Journal of Economic History*, 23, 1963, pp. 151–84.

16 S.G. Checkland and E.O.A. Checkland (eds), *The Poor Law Report of 1834* (Harmondsworth: Penguin, 1974), p. 36.

17 J.S. Mill, *Principles of Political Economy*, 5th edn, (London: Hodge, 1893), Vol. II, Bk V, ch. XI, p. 590.

18 J.S. Mill, *Principles of Political Economy*, Vol. I, p. 243.

19 Specifically by a subtle use of the tax system, see ibid., Vol. II, Book V, Chapters II, III, IV and V.

Chapter 3

1 See Sir Isaiah Berlin, 'Two Concepts of Liberty', in his *Four Essays on Liberty* (London: Oxford University Press, 1969).

2 See M. Freeden, *The New Liberalism* (Oxford: Blackwell, 1978).

3 R. Nettleship (ed.), *Green's Works* (London: Longman, 1888), Vol. III, p. 371.

4 Ibid., p. 376.

5 See B. Bosanquet, *The Philosophical Theory of the State* (London: Murray, 1899).

6 Herbert Spencer, *The Man versus the State* (London: Watt, 1940). First published in 1884.
7 J.A. Hobson, *Wealth* (London: Hodge, 1905).
8 L.T. Hobhouse, *Liberalism* (London: Oxford University Press, 1964).
9 L.T. Hobhouse, *Elements of Social Justice* (London: Allen and Unwin, 1922).
10 L.T. Hobhouse, *Liberalism*, p. 48.
11 L.T. Hobhouse, *Elements of Social Justice*, ch. VII.
12 See J. Clarke, A. Cochrane and Carol Smart (eds), *Ideologies of Welfare* (London: Hutchinson, 1987), pp. 161–9.
13 *Social Insurance and Allied Services*, Cmd 6404. (London: HMSO, 1942).
14 Ibid., p. 22.

Chapter 4

1 For methodological individualism, see K.R. Popper, *The Poverty of Historicism* (London: Routledge and Kegan Paul, 1957).
2 For an account of Pareto's work, see J. Schumpeter, *Ten Great Economists* (London: Oxford University Press, 1989).
3 See C.K. Rowley and A.T. Peacock, *Welfare Economics: A Liberal Restatement* (Oxford: Martin Robertson, 1975).
4 F.A. Hahn, *On the Concept of Equilibrium* (Cambridge: Cambridge University Press, 1974).
5 For an exposition and critique of 'market socialism' of this type, see D. Lavoie, *Rivalry and Central Planning* (Cambridge: Cambridge University Press, 1985).
6 Socialists tend to see 'market failure' as all-pervasive.
7 See especially, W.J. Baumol, *Welfare Economics and the Theory of the State*, 2nd edn (Cambridge, MA: Harvard University Press, 1967).
8 F.A. von Hayek, *The Mirage of Social Justice* (London: Routledge and Kegan Paul, 1976), ch. 8.
9 R. Coase, 'The Problem of Social Cost', *Journal of Law and Economics*, 3, 1960, pp. 1–44.
10 I. Kirzner, *Competition and Entrepreneurship* (Chicago: University of Chicago Press, 1973).
11 'The Principles of a Liberal Social Order', in F.A. von Hayek, *Studies in Philosophy, Politics and Economics* (London: Routledge and Kegan Paul, 1967), p. 153.
12 A. Sen, 'The Moral Standing of the Market', in Ellen Frankel Paul, Fred Miller and J. Paul (eds), *Ethics and Economics* (Oxford: Blackwell, 1985), p. 7.
13 M. Friedman, *Capitalism and Freedom* (Chicago: University of Chicago Press, 1962), p. 190.

14 See G. Gilder, *Wealth and Poverty* (New York: Basic Books, 1981).
15 See N.P. Barry, *The Invisible Hand in Economics and Politics* (London: Institute of Economic Affairs, 1988).
16 R. Sugden, *Who Cares?* (London: Institute of Economic Affairs, 1983), pp. 12–14.
17 Ibid., pp. 28–30.
18 Ibid., p. 24.
19 Ibid., p. 26.
20 A. Sen, *Poverty and Famines* (Oxford: Clarendon Press, 1981).
21 A good contemporary example is Ethiopia.
22 'The Profit Motive', *Lloyds Bank Review*, 1983, p. 12.

Chapter 5

1 D. Green, *Working Class Patients and the Medical Profession: Self-help in Britain from the Mid-Nineteenth Century to 1948* (London: Temple, 1985).
2 See Michael Taylor, *Anarchy, Community and Liberty* (Cambridge: Cambridge University Press, 1982).
3 Quoted in J. Kincaid, 'Titmuss', in P. Barker (ed.), *Founders of the Welfare State* (London: Heinemann, 1984), p. 116.
4 R. Goodin, *Protecting the Vulnerable* (Chicago: University of Chicago Press, 1985), p. 130.
5 R.M. Titmuss, *The Gift Relationship* (London: Allen and Unwin, 1970).
6 Ibid., p. 175.
7 See D. Collard, *Economics of Altruism* (London: Oxford University Press, 1978).
8 Quoted in A. Lynes, 'Beveridge', in *Founders of the Welfare State*, op. cit., p. 87.
9 K. Hoover and R. Plant, *Conservative Capitalism* (London: Routledge, 1989).
10 See M. Ricketts, *Lets into Leases* (London: Centre for Policy Studies, 1987).
11 A. Weale, *Political Theory and Social Policy* (London: Macmillan, 1983), p. 42.
12 Ibid., p. 28.
13 R. Plant, 'Needs, Agency and Rights', in Charles G. Sampford and D.J. Galligan (eds), *Law, Rights, and the Welfare State* (London: Croom Helm, 1986), p. 29.
14 R.M. Titmuss, 'Welfare Rights, Law and Discretion' in B. Abel-Smith and K. Titmuss (eds), *The Philosophy of Welfare* (London: Allen and Unwin, 1987), pp. 232–53.

15 'Are there any Natural Rights?', in A. Quinton (ed.), *Political Philosophy* (Oxford: Oxford University Press, 1967), pp. 55–6.
16 A. Hamlin, 'Rights, Efficiency and Commensurability', in *Law, Rights and the Welfare State*, op. cit., p. 97.
17 A. Gewirth, 'Private Philanthropy and Positive Rights', in Ellen Frankel Paul, Fred D. Miller, Jeffrey Paul and J. Ahrens (eds), *Beneficence, Philanthropy and the Public Good* (Oxford: Blackwell, 1987), p. 68.
18 D. Harris, *Justifying State Welfare* (Oxford: Blackwell, 1986), pp. 160–1.
19 T.H. Marshall, *Class, Citizenship, and Social Development* (Cambridge: Cambridge University Press, 1963).
20 D. King and J. Waldron, 'Welfare and Citizenship', *British Journal of Political Science*, 18, 1988, pp. 162–87.
21 D. Harris, *Justifying State Welfare*, op. cit., p. 51.

Chapter 6

1 R. Nozick, *Anarchy, State and Utopia* (Oxford: Blackwell, 1974), p. 22.
2 John Rawls, *A Theory of Justice* (Oxford: Blackwell, 1972).
3 Ibid., pp. 160–4.
4 G. Tullock, *The Economics of Wealth and Poverty* (Brighton: Wheatsheaf, 1985), ch. 1.
5 B. Barry, *The Liberal Theory of Justice* (London: Oxford University Press, 1973), ch. 8.
6 G. Brennan and J. Buchanan, *The Reason of Rules* (Cambridge: Cambridge University Press, 1986).
7 F.A. von Hayek, *The Constitution of Liberty* (London: Routledge and Kegan Paul, 1960), ch. 7.
8 F.A. von Hayek, *The Mirage of Social Justice* (London: Routledge and Kegan Paul, 1976), ch. 7.
9 See R. Plant, 'Needs, Agency, and Rights', in Charles G. Sampford and D.J. Galligan (eds), *Law, Rights and the Welfare State* (London: Croom Helm, 1986); also, K. Hoover and R. Plant, *Conservative Capitalism* (London: Routledge, 1989).
10 Hoover and Plant, *Conservative Capitalism*, op. cit., p. 214.
11 R.H. Tawney, *Equality* (London: Allen and Unwin, 1931).
12 J. Le Grand, *The Strategy of Equality* (London: Allen and Unwin, 1982).
13 Ibid., p. 46.
14 R. Goodin and J. Le Grand, *Not Only the Poor* (London: Allen and Unwin, 1987), ch. 4. In this book, Goodin and Le Grand use the instructive phrase 'beneficial involvement' to describe the relationship between the middle classes and the welfare state.

19 Nathan Glazer, *The Limits of Social Policy* (Cambridge, MA: Harvard University Press, 1988), p. 7.
20 Marvin Olasky, *The Tragedy of American Compassion* (Chicago: Regnery, 1992).
21 See D. Green, *Reinventing Civil Society* (London: Institute of Economic Affairs, 1993).
22 D. Green, ibid., ch. 7; M. Tanner, *The End of Welfare*, op. cit., p. 41.

Select Bibliography

There is no one general 'text' that treats welfare in its entirety, either from an analytical or historical perspective. For general introductions, the following are particularly useful:

Clarke, J., Cochrane, A. and Smart, C., *Ideologies of Welfare*, Routledge and Kegan Paul, London, 1987.

George, V. and Page, R., *Modern Thinkers on Welfare*. Prentice Hall/Harvester Wheatsheaf, London, 1995.

Goodin, R., *Political Theory and Public Policy*, University of Chicago Press, Chicago, 1985.

Griffin, J., *Well-being*, Clarendon Press, Oxford, 1986.

Hills, J. (ed.), *The State of Welfare*, Clarendon Press, Oxford, 1990.

Hills, J., *The Future of Welfare*, Joseph Rowntree Foundation, York, 1997.

Ignatieff, M., *The Needs of Strangers*, Chatto and Windus, London, 1984.

Pinker, R., *Social Theory and Public Policy*, Heinemann, London, 1971.

Pinker, R., *The Idea of Welfare*, Heinemann, London, 1979.

Plant, R., Lesser, M. and Taylor-Gooby, P., *Political Philosophy and Social Welfare*, Routledge and Kegan Paul, London, 1980.

Taylor-Gooby, P., *Social Theory and Social Welfare*, Allen and Unwin, London, 1984.

Weale, A. *Equality and Social Policy*, Routledge and Kegan Paul, London, 1978.

Weale, A., *Political Theory and Social Policy*, Macmillan, London, 1983.

The eighteenth- and nineteenth-century background, especially the emergence of utilitarianism as a *public* philosophy, is crucially important for the understanding of modern welfare theory. For admirable summaries, the following are especially recommended:

Ekuland, R., and Hebert, F., *A History of Economic Theory and Method*, McGraw Hill, New York, 1984.

Finer, S.E., *The Life and Times of Edwin Chadwick*, Oxford University Press, London, 1952.

Himmelfarb, G., *The Idea of Poverty: England in the Early Industrial Age*, Faber, London, 1984.

Letwin, S., *The Pursuit of Certainty*, Cambridge University Press, 1969.

Quinton, A., *Utilitarianism*, Clarendon Press, Oxford, 1978.

Robbins, L.C., *The Theory of Economic Policy in the Classical Economics*, Macmillan, London, 1952.

Schwarz, P., *The New Political Economy of John Stuart Mill*, Duke University Press, Durham, N.C., 1974.

Wilson, T. (ed.), *The Market and the State: Essays on Adam Smith*, Clarendon Press, Oxford, 1976.

There are a number of books on the communitarian reaction to nineteenth-century individualism. The best original text is:

Hobhouse, L.T., *Liberalism*, Oxford University Press, London, 1974. First published in 1911.

For commentaries on the period, see:

Freeden, M., *The New Liberalism*, Clarendon Press, Oxford, 1972.

Vincent, A. and Plant, R., *Philosophy, Politics and Citizenship*, Blackwell, Oxford, 1984.

The development of the British welfare state is traced in:

Bruce, M., *The Coming of the Welfare State*, Oxford University Press, London, 1965.

Fraser, D., *The Evolution of the British Welfare State*, Clarendon Press, Oxford, 1973.

Pope, R., Pratt, A. and Hoyle, B. (eds), *Social Welfare in Britain, 1885–1985*, Croom Helm, London, 1986.

Robson, W., *Welfare State and Welfare Society*, Allen & Unwin, London, 1976.

Contemporary philosophies of welfare are usually embedded in traditional ethical and political concepts. See the following:

Berlin, Sir I., *Four Essays on Liberty*, Oxford University Press, London, 1969.

Campbell, T., *Justice*, Macmillan, London, 1988.

Fried, C., *Right and Wrong*, Harvard University Press, Cambridge, MA, 1978.

Gerwirth, A., *Human Rights*, University of Chicago Press, Chicago, 1982.

Miller, D., *Social Justice*, Clarendon Press, Oxford, 1976.

Paul, E.F., Miller, F. and Paul, J., *Ethics and Economics*, Blackwell, Oxford, 1985.

Plant, R., *Modern Political Thought*, Blackwell, Oxford, 1991.

Raphael, D. D. (ed.), *Political Theory and the Rights of Man*, Macmillan, London, 1967.

Rawls, J., *A Theory of Justice*, Oxford University Press, London, 1972.

Sen, A.K., *Poverty and Famines*, Clarendon Press, Oxford, 1981.

Sen, A.K. and Williams, B. (eds) *Utilitarianism and Beyond*, Cambridge University Press, Cambridge, 1982.

Walzer, M., *Spheres of Justice*, Martin Robertson, Oxford, 1983.

Although much of the economics literature is highly technical and somewhat removed from the contemporary debate, an understanding of the political economy of welfare can be obtained from the following:

Atkinson, A.B., *Poverty and Social Security*, Harvester, Hemel Hempstead, 1989.

Atkinson, A.B., *Incomes and the Welfare State*, Cambridge University Press, Cambridge, 1996.

Barr, N., *The Economics of the Welfare State*, Allen & Unwin, London, 1993.

Baumol, W., *Welfare Economics and the Theory of the State*, Harvard University Press, Cambridge, MA, 1967.

Hamlin, A., *Ethics, Economics and the State*, Wheatsheaf, Brighton, 1986.

Le Grand, J. and Robinson, R., *The Economics of Social Problems*, Macmillan, London, 1984.

Ng, Y-K., *Welfare Economics*, Macmillan, London, 1979.

Pigou, A.C., *The Economics of Welfare*, Macmillan, London, 1920.

Rowley, C.K. and Peacock, A.T., *Welfare Economics: A Liberal Restatement*, Martin Robertson, Oxford, 1975.

Sugden, R., *The Economics of Rights, Welfare and Co-operation*, Blackwell, Oxford, 1986.

The welfare state is defended, the moral and economic claims of the market disputed, in:

Furness, N. and Tillon, T., *The Case for the Welfare State*, Indiana University Press, Bloomington, IN, 1976.

Goodin, R., *Protecting the Vulnerable*, University of Chicago Press, Chicago, 1985.

Goodin, R., *Reasons for Welfare*, Princeton University Press, Princeton, NJ, 1988.

Harrington, M., *The Other America*, Macmillan, New York, 1962.

Harris, D., *Justifying State Welfare*, Blackwell, Oxford, 1987.

Hoover, K. and Plant, R., *Conservative Capitalism*, Routledge, London, 1989.

Marshall, T.H., *Class, Citizenship and Social Development*, Allen &Unwin, London, 1963.

Marshall, T.H., *The Right to Welfare and Other Essays*, Heinemann, London, 1981.

Roemer, J., *Free to Lose*, Harvard University Press, Cambridge, MA, 1988.

Tawney, R. M., *Equality*, Allen & Unwin, London, 1931.

Titmus, R., *Essays on the Welfare State*, Allen & Unwin, London, 1958.

Titmus, R., *Commitment to Welfare*, Allen & Unwin, London, 1968.

Titmus, R., *The Gift Relationship*, Allen & Unwin, London, 1970.

Townsend, P., *Poverty in the United Kingdom*, Penguin, Harmondsworth, 1979.

Wilson, W.J., *The Truly Disadvantaged*, University of Chicago Press, Chicago, 1987.

Prominent among either sceptics or outright critics of the welfare state are:

Friedman, M., *Capitalism and Freedom*, University of Chicago Press, Chicago, 1962.

Friedman, M. and Friedman, R., *Free to Choose*, Penguin, Harmondsworth, 1981.

Gilder, G., *Wealth and Poverty*, Basic Books, New York, 1981.

Green, D., *Reinventing Civil Society*, Institute of Economic Affairs, London, 1993.

Mead, L., *The New Politics of Poverty*, Basic Books, New York, 1992.

Mead, L., *Beyond Entitlement: The Social Obligations of Citizenship*, Free Press, New York, 1986.

Murray, C., *Losing Ground: American Social Policy*, Basic Books, New York, 1984.

Murray, C., *Small Government and the Pursuit of Happiness*, Basic Books, New York, 1988.

Nozick, R., *Anarchy, State and Utopia*, Blackwell, Oxford, 1974.

Olasky, M., *The Tragedy of American Compassion*, Regnery, Chicago, 1992.

Skidelsky, R., *Beyond the Welfare State*, Social Market Foundation, London, 1997.

Sowell, T., *Knowledge and Decisions*, Basic Books, New York, 1980.

Sowell, T., *Markets and Minorities*, Basic Books, New York, 1981.

Sugden, R., *Who Cares?*, Institute of Economic Affairs, London, 1984.

Tanner, M., *The End of Welfare*, Cato Institute, Washington, D.C., 1996.
Tullock, G., *The Economics of Wealth and Poverty*, Wheatsheaf, Brighton, 1985.
von Hayek, F.A., *The Constitution of Liberty*, Routledge and Kegan Paul, London, 1960.

The following, although written by firm supporters of the welfare state, have a distinct relevance to its critique:

Goodin, R. and Le Grand, J., *Not Only the Poor: The Middle Classes and the Welfare State*, Allen & Unwin, London, 1987.
Le Grand, J., *The Strategy of Equality*, Allen & Unwin, London, 1982.

Index